T0185708

Managing Diabetes in Low Income Countries

Ivica Smokovski

Managing Diabetes in Low Income Countries

Providing Sustainable Diabetes Care
with Limited Resources

 Springer

Ivica Smokovski
Faculty of Medical Sciences
University Goce Delcev
Shtip
North Macedonia

University Clinic of Endocrinology
Diabetes and Metabolic Disorders
Skopje
North Macedonia

ISBN 978-3-030-51471-6   ISBN 978-3-030-51469-3   (eBook)
https://doi.org/10.1007/978-3-030-51469-3

© Springer Nature Switzerland AG 2021
This work is subject to copyright. All rights are reserved by the Publisher, whether the whole or part of the material is concerned, specifically the rights of translation, reprinting, reuse of illustrations, recitation, broadcasting, reproduction on microfilms or in any other physical way, and transmission or information storage and retrieval, electronic adaptation, computer software, or by similar or dissimilar methodology now known or hereafter developed.
The use of general descriptive names, registered names, trademarks, service marks, etc. in this publication does not imply, even in the absence of a specific statement, that such names are exempt from the relevant protective laws and regulations and therefore free for general use.
The publisher, the authors, and the editors are safe to assume that the advice and information in this book are believed to be true and accurate at the date of publication. Neither the publisher nor the authors or the editors give a warranty, expressed or implied, with respect to the material contained herein or for any errors or omissions that may have been made. The publisher remains neutral with regard to jurisdictional claims in published maps and institutional affiliations.

This Springer imprint is published by the registered company Springer Nature Switzerland AG
The registered company address is: Gewerbestrasse 11, 6330 Cham, Switzerland

Preface

We are already feeling the first impact of diabetes tsunami, and it is quite obvious that the coming waves are only going to get bigger. It is felt in the most developed countries and healthcare systems, and even they have a challenge managing the burden of diabetes, its complications, and the pressure on resources. But the impact is felt much stronger in the developing countries that already have difficulties in coping with the current healthcare issues and are definitely not prepared for the huge diabetes shock waves that are coming. And it is in developing countries where almost 80% of the people with diabetes are living, which only makes the problem even more complex.

The title of the book is *Managing Diabetes in Low-Income Countries—Providing Sustainable Diabetes Care with Limited Resources*. However, the term low-income countries, as used in the title and throughout the book, goes beyond the standard World Bank criteria of categorizing the countries. Please note while reading this book that low-income countries refer to the lower resource, developing countries, including both middle-income and low-income countries as defined by various authorities.

The book consists of nine chapters including the burden of diabetes prevalence, diabetes drivers, diabetes complications, available treatments, monitoring of metabolic control, diabetes education, e-Health solutions, nutrition, and diabetes prevention. The nine chapters illustrate the situation in developing compared to developed countries and propose initiatives for managing various diabetes challenges in a setting with limited resources.

Since this book is written in the middle of one of the greatest infectious pandemics humanity has ever faced, it is quite impressive to witness the immediate response to contain, diagnose, and treat COVID-19. It is spreading enormously fast, claiming lots of lives. It seems that humanity is at its best when dealing with imminent, global, fast-spreading danger. People have no problems changing their lifestyle they have had for years, in order to protect themselves, their family, beloved ones, and the whole humanity.

However, when we have to deal with another pandemic developing more insidiously over years, such as diabetes, we are reluctant to do even the slightest modification of our lifestyle. This results in a sad situation where diabetes is taking its massive toll.

There are countries in Europe, considered one of the most developed regions in the world, which are low-resource, developing, and with a very high diabetes prevalence. Those countries are struggling to balance between providing optimal diabetes care and not driving their healthcare systems into bankruptcy.

An example of a developing European country with limited resources is the Republic of North Macedonia, my home country that is mentioned on several occasions throughout the book. I have been honored to serve as a Medical Advisor for Diabetes Care to the Minister of Health in the period 2012–2016, and member of the National Diabetes Committee 2015–2017, so the examples presented in this book are my personal experiences and involvements.

Many aspects presented in this book and referring to developing countries could be equally relevant to the parts of population with diabetes living in developed countries. On the other hand, a minor part of diabetes population in developing countries has access to the highest level of diabetes care. The inequality in access to diabetes care within both developed and developing countries makes such categorization of countries largely vague.

Despite the title, this book truly seeks to present the challenges and potential solutions under circumstances with limited resources that could be found in both developed and developing countries.

It seems that after the global lockdown COVID-19 has caused, the struggle for providing sustainable diabetes care would become relevant not only for the developing but also for the countries that are currently considered as developed. The world would be different and there would certainly be more issues contesting for the limited healthcare resources.

It has been proven that even in a low-resource setting a lot could be done to fight diabetes and its complications. I would be feeling very fulfilled if this book has inspired you to take even a single initiative for curbing one of the biggest pandemics modern humanity has ever faced, diabetes.

And before you start reading, I would like to express immense gratitude to my family and my mentors, friends, and great endocrinologists, Prof Nanette Steinle and Prof Andrew Behnke without whom this book would not have been possible.

Skopje, Republic of North Macedonia   Ivica Smokovski
April 2020

Contents

About the Author

Ivica Smokovski, MD, PhD, is endocrinologist at the University Clinic of Endocrinology, Diabetes and Metabolic Disorders, Skopje, and Ass. Professor at the Faculty of Medical Sciences, University Goce Delcev, Shtip, Republic of North Macedonia.

Prof Smokovski has extensive experience in diabetes care from various positions: as a clinician at University Clinic, as a Medical Advisor in pharmaceutical industry, and as a Medical Advisor for Diabetes Care to the Minister of Health for 4 years (2012–2016).

He has been instrumental in instituting and serving as a member of the first National Diabetes Committee, responsible for development of National Diabetes Plan and National Diabetes Care Guidelines and monitoring the implementation of policies and guidelines.

Prof Smokovski had a key role in the founding of National e-Health System related to diabetes care, covering the total population of the country across all healthcare levels. He has been involved in the implementation of the diabetes care activities presented in this book.

Prof Smokovski has published the state-of-the-art article "Diabetes care in the Republic of Macedonia: Challenges and opportunities," the first comprehensive overview of the situation with diabetes in the Republic of North Macedonia, estimated to have one of the highest diabetes prevalence in Europe.

In addition, he has published the article "First stratified diabetes prevalence data for Republic of Macedonia derived from the National e-Health System," the first analysis of diabetes data from the National e-Health System.

Prof Smokovski is a National Representative of EPMA (European Association for Predictive, Preventive and Personalized Medicine), member of Presidency of the National Scientific Association of Endocrinologists and Diabetologists, and President of the Scientific Committee of National Diabetes Days.

He was responsible for the introduction of Neonatal Cardiac Surgery, US-MK Exchange Physician Program, and Balanced Score Card in public healthcare institutions of the country, and he served as a President of the National Council of Residencies and Fellowships in the period 2013–2016.

He was the first winner of the Prize for Best Published Article in the *Journal of Doctor's Chamber* of Macedonia in 2014 and a winner of the Donnell D. Etzwiler International Scholar Award 2020.

Prof Smokovski is author of the Regional Project awarded two-years grant (2019–2021) by the International Diabetes Federation, titled "Estimation of Stratified Total Diabetes & Pre-Diabetes Prevalence in Western Balkan Countries".

He has been invited to lecture at numerous domestic and international diabetes medical events.

Abbreviations

ADA	American Diabetes Association
AGP	Ambulatory glucose profile
ASCVD	Atherosclerotic cardiovascular disease
BG	Blood glucose
BGM	Blood glucose meter
BMI	Body mass index
CDC	Centers for Disease Control and Prevention
CGM	Continuous glucose monitoring
CKD	Chronic kidney disease
CVD	Cardiovascular disease
DCCT	Diabetes Control and Complications Trial
DKA	Diabetic ketoacidosis
DPP	Diabetes Prevention Program
DPP-4i	Dipeptidyl peptidase-4 inhibitor
EDIC	Epidemiology of Diabetes Interventions and Complications
EHCI	European Healthcare Consumer Index
EHR	Electronic healthcare record
FDA	Food and Drug Administration
FPG	Fasting plasma glucose
GDM	Gestational diabetes mellitus
GDP	Gross domestic product
GLP-1RA	Glucagon-like peptide-1 receptor agonist
GMI	Glucose Management Indicator
GNI	Gross national income
GP	General practitioner
GV	Glycemic variability
HbA1c	Glycated hemoglobin A1c
HDL	High density lipoprotein cholesterol
HHS	Hyperglycemic hyperosmolar state
HIV/AIDS	Human immunodeficiency virus/Acquired immunodeficiency syndrome

ICU	Intensive care unit
IDF	International Diabetes Federation
IFG	Impaired fasting glucose
IGT	Impaired glucose tolerance
INR	Indian rupee
isCGM	intermittently scanned continuous glucose monitoring
ISO	International Organization for Standardization
LDL	Low-density lipoprotein cholesterol
LMICs	Low- and middle-income countries
MARD	Mean absolute relative difference
MKD	Macedonian denar
MU	Mega units
NAFLD	Non-alcoholic fatty liver disease
NCD	Noncommunicable disease
NeHS	National e-Health System
NGSP	National Glycohemoglobin Standardization Program
NHS	National Health Service
OAD	Oral antidiabetic drug
OGTT	Oral glucose tolerance test
PG	Plasma glucose
PPG	Postprandial glycemia
PPPM	Predictive, preventive, and personalized medicine
PVD	Peripheral vascular disease
QoL	Quality of life
SDEP	Structured Diabetes Education Program
SGLT2i	Sodium glucose cotransporter 2 inhibitor
SMBG	Self-monitoring of blood glucose
TAR	Time above range
TBR	Time below range
TIR	Time in range
UACR	Urinary albumin creatinine ratio
UK	United Kingdom
UKPDS	UK Prospective Diabetes Study
UKPDS-PTM	UK Prospective Diabetes Study Post-trial Monitoring
UHC	Universal Health Coverage
US	United States
USD	United States Dollars
WHO	World Health Organization

Chapter 1
Burden of Diabetes Prevalence

It is now evident that we are living in a world of diabetes pandemic—despite the scientifically sound estimates, worldwide diabetes prevalence has been exceeding even the most pessimistic projections from the past. If we go back in history, it was estimated in 2004 that diabetes prevalence in 2030 would reach 366 million people [1]. What actually happened was that the prevalence of 366 million people with diabetes was already reached in 2011, 19 years earlier than initially predicted [2]. According to the latest projections, there would be 578 million people with diabetes in 2030, almost 60% more of what was estimated 15 years ago (Fig. 1.1) [1, 2].

Exponential rise of diabetes prevalence can also be observed from the historical data in the past 20 years. The global estimate of the total diabetes prevalence, including both diagnosed and undiagnosed cases in the age group 20–79 years, was 151 million in 2000; rising to 194 million in 2003; 246 million in 2006; 285 million in 2009; 366 million in 2011; 382 million in 2013; 415 million in 2015; and 425 million in 2017 [2].

According to the latest estimates from the International Diabetes Federation (IDF) Diabetes Atlas, approximately 463 million people in the age group 20–79 year were living with diabetes in 2019, equaling to 9.3% of the world's population in this age group [2]. The total number is predicted to rise to 578 million by 2030 (prevalence of 10.2%); and 700 million by 2045 (prevalence of 10.9%) [2].

The number of people with diabetes is extraordinary, and the question is what places so many people in this category. Diabetes mellitus is defined as Fasting Plasma Glucose (FPG) $\geq$7.0 mmol/L (126 mg/dL); or 2-h Plasma Glucose (PG) $\geq$11.1 mmol/L (200 mg/dL) during Oral Glucose Tolerance Test (OGTT, glucose load containing the equivalent of 75 g anhydrous glucose dissolved in water); or HbA1c $\geq$6.5% (48 mmol/mol) in a laboratory using a method that is NGSP certified and standardized to the DCCT assay; or if an individual presents with classic symptoms of hyperglycemia and a random plasma glucose $\geq$11.1 mmol/L (200 mg/dL) [3].

© Springer Nature Switzerland AG 2021
I. Smokovski, *Managing Diabetes in Low Income Countries*,
https://doi.org/10.1007/978-3-030-51469-3_1

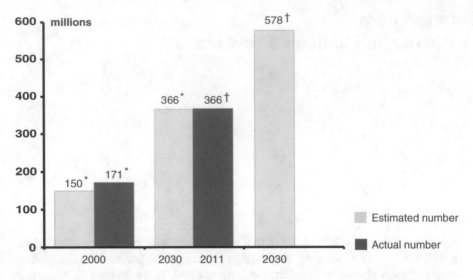

Fig. 1.1 Estimated and actual number of people with diabetes, data adapted from [1, 2] (asterisk) Wild et al. (2014), (dagger) IDF Diabetes Atlas (2019)

Diabetes mellitus is a heterogeneous entity and is classified into type 1 diabetes (autoimmune beta-cell destruction resulting in absolute insulin deficiency), type 2 diabetes (progressive loss of adequate beta-cell insulin secretion due to insulin resistance), and gestational diabetes mellitus (GDM, diabetes diagnosed during pregnancy) [3].

Other causes are less frequent, such as monogenic diabetes syndromes (neonatal diabetes and maturity-onset diabetes of the young), diseases of the exocrine pancreas (cystic fibrosis, pancreatic cancer, pancreatitis, pancreatectomy), and drug- or chemical-induced diabetes (glucocorticoid use, treatment of HIV/AIDS, or after organ transplantation) [3].

Furthermore, the burden of diabetes is not only the magnitude of people diagnosed with diabetes by any of the criteria above, but also the huge number of people with diabetes who are not diagnosed. It is estimated that 1 in 2 people with diabetes is undiagnosed; or, out of the total 463 million in 2019, 232 million people with diabetes were undiagnosed [2]. It means that for every person with known diabetes, there is another one yet to be found, tested, diagnosed and adequately treated. There are many people in the community who are not aware to be living with diabetes. Unfortunately, many of those who have diabetes, but are not diagnosed, initially present with diabetes complications that are even more difficult and costly to treat.

The vast majority of people affected by diabetes are in their most productive years. There were 351.7 million people with diabetes in 2019, or 75% of the total number, who were of working age from 20 to 64 years [2]. This number is expected to increase to 417.3 million by 2030, and 486.1 million by 2045 [2]. The magnitude of people with diabetes in their working age has an immense impact on the economies globally. The impact is felt much stronger if the economy is weaker, as in the lower resource countries.

Diabetes is among the top ten causes of mortality in the adult population worldwide [4]. Latest estimates for 2019 suggest that it has caused 4.2 million deaths worldwide in the age group 20–79 years [2]. For this reason, it is often said that diabetes has killed more people after World War II, than both World Wars combined. It is evident that we are still counting the increasing number of casualties, with no signs of flattening the curve in the near future. The fight against diabetes has frequently been labeled by some prominent IDF leaders as the invisible World War III that is affecting the whole humanity. If people with diabetes are population of a separate country, it would be the third largest country in the world, right after China and India, and much bigger than the United States (US). Almost one percent of this country would be dying annually.

The steep rise in diabetes prevalence discussed above has mainly been attributed to the increased prevalence of type 2 diabetes [2]. Type 2 diabetes is estimated to account for more than 95% of all cases of diabetes globally. Not only the absolute number, but also the proportion of people with type 2 diabetes is increasing worldwide.

When facing pandemics of different nature, such as the recent infectious COVID-19 pandemic, that are contagious, spreading fast and globally, we see whole societies taking immediate action, building up hospital and ICU capacities, governments discussing nationwide strategies and solutions. The life of whole countries changes over night. The question is why we are not seeing this sense of urgency when facing the diabetes pandemic, claiming multiple times more lives than the recent infectious pandemic with COVID-19?

The answer could be the insidious course of diabetes that lasts for years before it is even diagnosed. We are not talking about days or weeks of incubation, but often about years for diabetes to develop. And when something is explosive in nature, as in infectious pandemics, we don't have difficulties modifying our lifestyle abruptly, adapting to the new circumstances. We are afraid that the healthcare system will not respond to the overwhelming number of infectious cases. However, when something develops slowly over the course of years, people seem to be reluctant to modify their lifestyle to delay it or prevent it. That may explain why the challenge of flattening the curve of diabetes prevalence is so burdensome.

When we talk about the burden of diabetes prevalence, we also have to think of the diabetes related complications. It is well established that people with diabetes have increased risk for coronary artery disease, stroke, congestive heart failure, peripheral vascular disease, retinopathy, nephropathy, and neuropathy, among the most common [2, 3]. Less recognized, however, equally important, are the increased prevalence of depression, erectile dysfunction, or functional disability [2, 3].

Cardiovascular diseases, leading cause of morbidity and mortality worldwide, are two to four times more common in people with diabetes compared to people with no diabetes [2, 3]. Diabetes remains the leading cause of the new cases of blindness among adults, and the leading cause of end-stage renal failure requiring dialysis [2]. The enormous impact of diabetes related complications will be discussed in more detail in the following chapters.

Diabetes has been a major healthcare issue for the lower resource, developing countries. Developing countries include low-income countries, with Gross National Income (GNI) per capita of USD 1,025 or less, and middle-income countries, with GNI per capita between USD 1,025 and USD 12,375 in 2018 [5]. Developed, high-income countries are those with GNI per capita of USD 12,376 or more in 2018 [5].

Developing countries are sometimes referred to as LMICs, or Low and Middle Income Countries. It is estimated that only 15% of the world population lives in developed countries and the remaining majority lives in developing, lower resource countries.

The trend of rising prevalence of type 2 diabetes in both developed and developing countries can be attributed to ageing, sedentary lifestyle and increased calories intake, resulting in overweight, obesity and insulin resistance. In 2019, 310.3 million people with diabetes were living in urban areas (prevalence of 10.8%), compared to 152.6 million in rural areas (prevalence of 7.2%) [2]. Number of people with diabetes in urban areas is expected to increase to 415.4 million (prevalence of 11.9%) in 2030, and to 538.8 million (prevalence of 12.5%) in 2045, as a result of the global migration from rural to urban areas [2]. The urbanization is more intensive in developing countries, and could lead to even sharper increase in diabetes prevalence in those countries.

Earlier diagnosis, treatment and reduction of premature complications and mortality additionally contribute to the increased diabetes prevalence, due to the better survival of people with diabetes [2]. Diagnosing type 2 diabetes at an earlier age in recent years also contributes to the increase of diabetes prevalence.

While the prevalence of diabetes becomes less steep in higher resource parts of the world, it is expected to explode in the years to come in the lower resource countries. It further aggravates the situation with the already scarce healthcare resources in developing countries, and poses additional challenges for the healthcare authorities to prioritize and adequately allocate the limited resources.

Healthcare systems of developing countries have already been struggling with the existing healthcare issues and have certainly not been prepared to face the approaching diabetes tsunami. Most of these countries have not been able to provide the currently recommended standard diabetes treatment or glucose monitoring supplies to the already diagnosed people with diabetes. The economic meltdown from the recent global pandemic with COVID-19 would only aggravate the financial situation in the healthcare systems of developing countries.

It is striking that in 2019, 79% of adults with diabetes, or 367.8 million (prevalence of 9.0%) were living in developing countries, compared to 95.2 million (prevalence of 10.4%) in developed countries (Fig. 1.2) [2]. Unstoppable diabetes tsunami is coming for the developing countries which could easily be realized from the projections for 2030 and 2045, if current trends are not changed.

In 2030, it is estimated that 82% of the total number of people with diabetes will be coming from developing countries [2]. Estimated 470.1 million people with

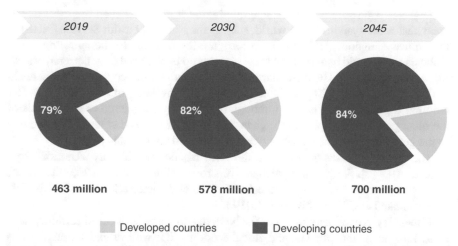

Fig. 1.2 Diabetes prevalence in developed and developing countries, 2019–2045, data adapted from [2]

diabetes will be living in developing (prevalence of 10.0%), compared to 107.9 million in developed countries (prevalence of 11.4%) (Fig. 1.2) [2].

In 2045, it is estimated that 84% of the total number of people with diabetes will be coming from developing countries [2]. Estimated 587.6 million people with diabetes will be living in developing (prevalence of 10.8%), compared to 112.4 million in developed countries (prevalence of 11.9%) (Fig. 1.2) [2].

Diabetes prevalence is projected to increase by 51% from 2019 to 2045 worldwide—from 463 million in 2019, to 700 million in 2045 [2]. This rise is largely due to the increase in low- to middle-income regions, such as in Africa (except North Africa) by 143%, Middle East and North Africa by 96%, South East Asia by 74%, and South and Central America by 55% [2].

We should never forget how bad we have been in predicting diabetes prevalence. No matter how tremendous those numbers may appear, all historical projections have so far resulted in significant underestimation of the diabetes prevalence. Therefore, we should only consider future estimates as the most conservative ones.

The proportion of people with undiagnosed diabetes is also higher in low-income (66.8%, 9.7 million) and middle-income (52.6%, 185.8 million), compared to high-income countries (38.3%, 36.4 million) [2]. Expected improvement of diagnostic rates in developing countries would result in additional number of people with diagnosed diabetes that the healthcare systems have to cope with.

Financial burden of diabetes and related complications has been overwhelming for the healthcare systems across the world. It is estimated that diabetes caused at least USD 760 billion of healthcare expenditure in 2019, which is approximately 10% of the total spending on adult healthcare [2]. This figure is projected to rise to USD 825 billion in 2030, and USD 845 billion in 2045 [2]. If indirect costs are added, as explained in the following chapters, total diabetes related costs become even higher.

Diabetes pandemic is of such magnitude that it threatens even the most developed healthcare systems in the world, such as the National Health Service (NHS) in the United Kingdom (UK). Some experts predict that due to the spiraling costs, diabetes alone could bankrupt the NHS and should be declared as a 'national crisis'. Mass media from the UK have alarmed that the number of people with diabetes in the UK has doubled in 20 years, due to the rise in prevalence of type 2 diabetes [6]. Another frightening fact is that, although traditionally considered as a diagnosis of the older population, type 2 diabetes is more often diagnosed at an earlier age due to the growing prevalence of obesity in children and adolescents [6].

The cost of diabetes treatment in the NHS has doubled in only a decade, from 2008 to 2018 [6]. Furthermore, diabetes was responsible for almost 26,000 cases of premature mortality annually in the UK [6]. Total diabetes related cost in the UK was estimated at USD 17 billion in 2019 [2].

If there is a risk of bankruptcy of the NHS due to diabetes, it could certainly have a huge impact on the total UK and global economy. It is well validated that diabetes is the largest contributor to healthcare costs, not only in the UK, but also in the rest of Europe, exerting huge pressure on the already stretched healthcare resources.

It is no surprise that diabetes is one of the costliest conditions in the most developed country of the world, the US. The Center for Disease Control and Prevention (CDC) Report from 2020 estimated that more than 1 in 10 US adults—about 34.1 million—have either type 1 or type 2 diabetes, and 7.3 million of them are undiagnosed [7].

Total diabetes related health expenditure in the US in 2019 was estimated at USD 294.6 billion, the largest amount spent on diabetes by a single country [2]. It is three times more than the diabetes related health expenditure of China, which occupies the second place and has four times more people with diabetes than the US. It is estimated that cost to the economy of diabetes related premature deaths in the US was USD 19.9 billion annually, and a total of USD 90 billion was indirectly lost due to diabetes [2, 8].

Above grave examples of the diabetes impact on the most developed countries illustrate the potential it has to collapse the healthcare systems of the developing, lower resource countries. An example of a developing country struggling with one of the highest diabetes prevalence in Europe is the Republic of North Macedonia, located in South East Europe, with an estimated population of 2.06 million [9]. The increasing prevalence of type 2 diabetes in the past three decades has been alarming and had a significant impact on the healthcare system in the country.

The estimated total diabetes prevalence, of both diagnosed and undiagnosed cases, in the Republic of North Macedonia was approximately 80,000 people in 2004 [9]. Diabetes prevalence has more than doubled in only 15 years, and the latest estimate of total diabetes prevalence was 175,100 in 2019 [2].

Both diabetes national and age-adjusted prevalence in the Republic of North Macedonia were higher compared to Europe as a region. Diabetes national prevalence in adults 20–79 years in 2019 was estimated at 11.2%, compared to 8.9% in Europe [2]. Diabetes age-adjusted comparative prevalence (20–79 years) in 2019 was estimated at 9.3%, compared to 6.3% in Europe [2].

Table 1.1 Basic diabetes data for the Republic of North Macedonia, data adapted from [2, 9, 10]

Total population	2,058,539
Diabetes national prevalence (20–79 years) (2019)	11.2%
Diabetes age-adjusted comparative prevalence (20–79 years) (2019)	9.3%
Total number of people with diabetes (diagnosed and undiagnosed) (2019)	175,100
People with diagnosed diabetes (2015)	84,568
People with diabetes on insulin treatment (2015)	37,011 (43.8% of diagnosed cases)
People with type 1 diabetes (2015)	2,300 (2.7% of diagnosed cases)
Women/men with diagnosed diabetes (% prevalence) (2015)	48,449 (4.6%)/36,119 (3.4%)
Urban/rural population with diagnosed diabetes (% prevalence) (2015)	59,586 (3.6%)/24,982 (5.6%)

It was estimated there were 2,300 people with type 1 diabetes in the Republic of North Macedonia in 2015, or 2.7% of all diagnosed cases [9]. The Republic of North Macedonia is considered a 'cold spot' for type 1 diabetes in Europe with a low incidence rate [9]. On the other hand, the prevalence of type 2 diabetes in the country is strikingly high. Basic diabetes data for the Republic of North Macedonia are presented in Table 1.1 [2, 9, 10].

Diabetes has been a huge healthcare and socio-economic burden for the Republic of North Macedonia. National diabetes prevalence data have been of utmost importance for the policy makers, healthcare authorities, healthcare providers, and patient organizations. Nevertheless, it is interesting that until recently, there were only external estimates of the diabetes prevalence for the country. Those estimates were based on extrapolations of diabetes prevalence from other countries in the region, as there were no reliable data sources for the national diabetes prevalence [10]. Using extrapolated data for estimation of diabetes prevalence has been common for most of the developing countries, lacking their own, good quality epidemiological data [2].

It was also interesting that up to the latest, ninth edition of IDF Diabetes Atlas, the same age-adjusted (20–79 years) comparative prevalence of 10.1% was reported not only for the Republic of North Macedonia, but also for the other countries from the region with no own data, such as Albania, Bosnia and Herzegovina, Montenegro and Serbia [10, 11].

Those estimates were based upon the extrapolation of diabetes prevalence in geographically close countries with high quality data for diabetes prevalence, such as Croatia, Cyprus, Greece, Slovenia and Turkey [10, 11]. However, not all of those reference countries, although geographically close, share similar dietary and lifestyle patterns with the Republic of North Macedonia and the other countries with no own data [10].

First step for the developing countries is to know their own diabetes prevalence of diagnosed cases, as precisely as possible. In other words, if we are talking about fighting a war against diabetes, we have to know the strength of our enemy in every single country, including the ones with limited resources. Additionally, it is not sufficient only to know the total number of diagnosed cases, but also to know the stratification of those cases by age, gender and place of living, urban or rural. This information is of great value for explaining the prevalence and helps for planning of future activities.

After determining the prevalence of diagnosed cases, it would be beneficial to know the prevalence of undiagnosed cases through a national epidemiological study. If the prevalence of diagnosed and undiagnosed cases is known, the total diabetes prevalence could be calculated, as well as the diagnostic rate for the country.

The next thing every developing country should consider is mapping the network of diabetes care services provided across the national healthcare system. In the case of the Republic of North Macedonia, diabetes care services are provided across all three healthcare levels, primary, secondary and tertiary. Around 1,600 primary care physicians are involved in the screening, diagnosing and treating people with type 2 diabetes with oral antidiabetic medication. In addition, there are 41 Diabetes Centers with around 120 specialists (Endocrinologists, Diabetologists, Internists) which are functional units at secondary level where further diabetes care is provided, including prescription of insulin treatment and other novel injectable (e.g. GLP-1RA) and non-injectable (e.g. DPP-4i, SGLT2i) diabetes medications. Finally, there is one institution at tertiary level, the University Clinic of Endocrinology, Diabetes and Metabolic Disorders in the capital of Skopje. If not in possession of those basic metrics, any war against diabetes is predestined to fail.

The first comprehensive, stratified diabetes prevalence data derived from the National e-Health system in the Republic of North Macedonia with a cut-off date 20-July-2015, were published in 2018 [10]. These first actual data on the national diabetes prevalence discovered certain differences compared to the previously reported extrapolations [10]. Diabetes prevalence data of diagnosed cases were stratified by age, gender and place of living [10].

Latest, ninth edition of IDF Diabetes Atlas used the first stratified, national data of diagnosed cases derived from the National e-Health System (NeHS), for the estimates of total diabetes prevalence for the Republic of North Macedonia in 2019 [2]. Those are the first results without extrapolation of data from regional countries, and are considered more accurate than the estimates from the previous versions of the IDF Diabetes Atlas.

The Republic of North Macedonia was recognized in the latest IDF Diabetes Atlas from 2019, as one out of only 12 countries worldwide having a diabetes prevalence study conducted within the past 5 years [2]. Hence, it is possible even for a developing country with limited resources to report the national diabetes prevalence, at least of diagnosed cases.

From the first stratified analysis of diabetes prevalence it was found that genders were evenly distributed in the total population of the Republic of North Macedonia, whereas the majority of the population lives in urban municipalities (78.9%), mimicking the global distribution of population [10].

The total number of diagnosed cases was 84,568; of those 36,119 men (42.7%) and 48,449 women (57.3%) (Table 1.1) [10]. Mean age of all diagnosed diabetes

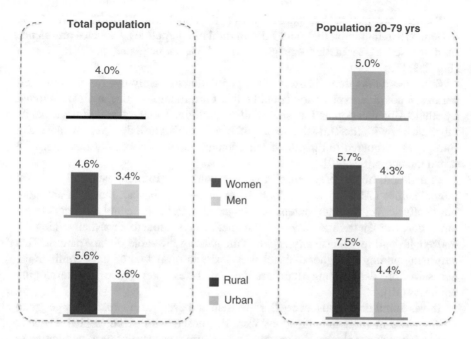

Fig. 1.3 Diabetes prevalence of diagnosed cases in the Republic of North Macedonia, total population and population 20–79 years [10]

cases was 62.6 ± 12.5 years. It was reported that prevalence of diagnosed cases in the total population was 4.0% with the highest prevalence in the age group 60–79 years, followed by groups 80 years or older, 40–59 years, 20–39 years, and below 20 years (Fig. 1.3) [10]. This is in accordance with the global estimates of increasing diabetes prevalence towards older age groups [2].

The prevalence of diagnosed cases was higher in women compared to men in the total population (4.6% vs 3.4%) (Fig. 1.3) [10]. This was a surprising result in contrast to the global estimates of higher prevalence in men (9.6%) than in women (9.0%) in 2019, but also in the future projections (10.4% and 10.0% in 2030, and 11.1% and 10.8% in 2045, in men and women, respectively) [2].

From the study, the total number of diagnosed cases was higher in urban ($n = 59,586$) compared to rural municipalities ($n = 24,982$); however, the prevalence of diagnosed cases was higher in rural compared to urban municipalities (5.6% vs 3.6%) across all age groups, except for the age group below 20 years, where the majority of diagnosed cases (99.1%) were from urban municipalities (Fig. 1.3) [10]. This was also in contrast to the global trends of higher diabetes prevalence in urban compared to rural areas [2, 10].

The process of urbanization has been very intensive in the Republic of North Macedonia in the past 50 years with significant migration from rural to urban municipalities. Higher diabetes prevalence of diagnosed cases in rural municipalities contradicts the established views of higher diabetes prevalence associated with urbanization [2, 10].

Diabetes prevalence of diagnosed cases in the population 20–79 years was 5.0%, 4.4% in urban municipalities, and 7.5% in rural municipalities. Diabetes prevalence of diagnosed cases in this age group was 4.3% in men and 5.7% in women (Fig. 1.3) [10].

Since more than three quarters of the population currently live in urban munici-palities, a possible explanation could be that rural municipalities, mainly inhibited by ethnic Albanian population, share cultural, religious, dietary, and lifestyle habits more closely with the Turkish population, having the highest diabetes prevalence in Europe, as compared to the ethnic Macedonian population, mainly inhabiting the urban municipalities [10].

In addition, higher prevalence in women compared to men, especially in rural municipalities (7.0% vs 4.3%), could be explained by the fact that men are more physically active, and more intensively engaged in agriculture and farming. On the other side, women traditionally stay at home, being responsible for maintaining the households and less physically active while sharing the same dietary pattern. This surprising finding of higher diabetes prevalence in rural women only confirms the necessity of determining the stratified diabetes prevalence in developing countries [10].

It was found that almost every third woman and every fifth man in the age group 60–79 years in rural municipalities were diagnosed with diabetes [10]. Possible reason for such a high prevalence could be the limited access of rural population to Diabetes Centers which are located exclusively in urban municipalities, where activities are directed also towards diabetes prevention [10].

The Republic of North Macedonia could still be considered a 'cold spot' for type 1 diabetes in Europe, as only 549 individuals (0.6% of all diagnosed cases) were below the age of 20 years, with equal gender distribution, and all but one individual coming from urban municipalities. This finding further strengthens the importance of environmental factors arising from urban municipalities in initiation of autoim-munity in type 1 diabetes.

Taking into account the estimated high diabetes prevalence and exorbitant related costs, diabetes has been posing a serious threat, not only to the national healthcare system, but to the society as a whole. As an illustration, cost of insulin and related supplies, test strips, glucagon, insulin pumps and ancillaries; not including the cost of oral antidiabetic drugs, was 40% of the total cost of all non-hospital medications covered by the Healthcare Insurance Fund and Government Programs in 2014 (Fig. 1.4) [9, 10].

In order to manage the burden of diabetes prevalence, especially in lower resource countries, numerous activities need to be undertaken. Those activities have to be endorsed by the top policy decision makers in order to be implemented.

Examples of activities undertaken at institutional level to address the diabetes burden in the Republic of North Macedonia, include: (1) adoption of National Diabetes Plan at the level of Ministry of Health, strategic document describing the current situation and the proposed activities on diabetes treatment, education, pre-vention; (2) addition of diabetes as a specifically designated medical condition in the Law on Healthcare; (3) adoption of international guidelines for diabetes care as National Diabetes Care guidelines, published in the Official Journal of the country

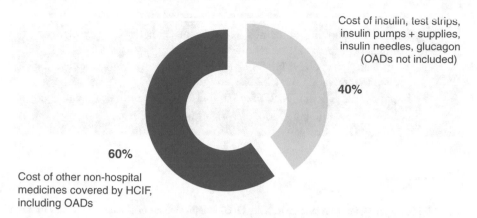

Cost of insulin, test strips,
insulin pumps + supplies,
insulin needles, glucagon
(OADs not included)

40%

60%

Cost of other non-hospital
medicines covered by HCIF,
including OADs

Fig. 1.4 Cost of insulin and related supplies as a percentage of the total cost for non-hospital reimbursed medications [10]. *OAD* Oral Antidiabetic Drugs, *HCIF* Healthcare Insurance Fund

where laws are published, to ensure adherence by all stakeholders; (4) formation of a National Diabetes Committee, body for monitoring of adherence to the National Diabetes Care guidelines; (5) creation of NeHS to monitor the diagnosis and treatment of people with diabetes [10, 12, 13].

These activities comply with the World Health Organization (WHO) recommendations for establishing National Diabetes Plans and providing Universal Healthcare Coverage (UHC) by 2030, as well as reduction of premature death from noncommunicable diseases (NCDs), including diabetes, by 25% by 2025 [2, 14].

The findings from the national analysis in a small, severely affected, lower resource country, such as the Republic of North Macedonia, further strengthen the need that each developing country should be in possession of its real-world, stratified, diabetes prevalence data, instead of using extrapolations.

The analyses of the national, stratified diabetes prevalence were performed with very limited financial resources, confirming it is possible to generate numerous diabetes related reports in a setting of a lower resource country, if the NeHS is in place.

What should be done to manage the burden of diabetes prevalence in developing countries?
Each developing country should …

- … know its numbers—as a minimum, the prevalence of diagnosed cases, stratified by age, gender and place of living, urban or rural;
- … consider epidemiological study to find the prevalence of undiagnosed diabetes cases;
- … map the diabetes care services across all healthcare levels;
- … have a National Diabetes Plan, and consider designating diabetes as a specific medical condition in the laws;

- ... adopt international guidelines as National Diabetes Care guidelines, requiring adherence by all stakeholders;
- ... form a national body, National Diabetes Committee, overseeing the adherence to the National Diabetes Care guidelines;
- ... implement a national, centralized, integrated electronic healthcare system covering the total population across all healthcare levels.

References

1. Wild S, Roglic G, Green A, Sicree R, King H. Global prevalence of diabetes: estimates for the year 2000 and projections for 2030. Diabetes Care. 2004;27:1047–53.
2. International Diabetes Federation. IDF Diabetes Atlas. 9th ed. Brussels: International Diabetes Federation; 2019.
3. American Diabetes Association. Standards of medical care in diabetes 2020. Diabetes Care. 2020;43(1):s1–212.
4. World Health Organization. The top 10 causes of death. 24 May 2018. https://www.who.int/news-room/fact-sheets/detail/the-top-10-causes-of-death. Accessed 13 March 2020.
5. The World Bank Group Data. Classifying countries by income. https://datatopics.worldbank.org/world-development-indicators/stories/the-classification-of-countries-by-income.html. Accessed 15 March 2020.
6. Express.co.uk: Diabetes warning: epidemic may 'bankrupt the NHS'. 2019. https://www.express.co.uk/life-style/health/1201749/Diabetes-warning-NHS-latest-migrants. Accessed 01 April 2020.
7. Centers for Disease Control and Prevention. National Diabetes Statistics Report, 2020. Atlanta, GA: Centers for Disease Control and Prevention, U.S. Department of Health and Human Services; 2020.
8. American Diabetes Association Statement. Economic costs of diabetes in the U.S. in 2017. Diabetes Care. 2018;41(5):917–28.
9. Smokovski I, Milenkovic T, Trapp C, Mitov A. Diabetes care in the Republic of Macedonia: challenges and opportunities. Ann Global Health. 2015;81(6):792–802.
10. Smokovski I, Milenkovic T, Cho HN. First stratified diabetes prevalence data for Republic of Macedonia derived from the National e-Health System. Diabetes Res Clin Pract. 2018;143:179–83.
11. International Diabetes Federation. IDF Diabetes Atlas. 8th ed. Brussels: International Diabetes Federation; 2017.
12. Ministry of Health. Law on the healthcare. Off J Repub Macedonia. 2015;10:12–88.
13. Ministry of Health. Guideline on healthcare related to the treatment and control of type 2 diabetes. Off J Repub Macedonia. 2015;40:15–34.
14. World Health Organization. Noncommunicable diseases: Campaign for action – meeting the NCD targets. Know the NCD targets. https://www.who.int/beat-ncds/take-action/targets/en/. Accessed 05 April 2020.

Chapter 2
Diabetes Drivers

Ageing population is one of the main drivers for the rise of diabetes prevalence worldwide. People are living longer, thereby increasing their chances to develop diabetes. In addition, people diagnosed with diabetes are also living longer due to the improved treatment of hyperglycemia and diabetes complications. As already mentioned, type 2 diabetes has recently been more often diagnosed at an earlier age, increasing the overall type 2 diabetes prevalence through longer survival.

There is a considerable difference if we compare developed and developing countries in terms of life expectancy. Life expectancy at birth in low-income countries is estimated at 62.7 years, 18.1 years lower than in high-income countries, estimated at 80.8 years [1]. Most of the people who die in high-income countries are of old age; however, almost one third of mortality in low-income countries is in very young children, under the age of 5 years [1].

The differences in life expectancy between women and men are smaller in low-income countries compared to high-income countries [1]. Currently, communicable diseases and maternal conditions contribute most to differences in life expectancy between women and men in low-income countries, whereas NCDs, including diabetes, contribute most to the life expectancy differences in high-income countries [1].

Life expectancy has been increasing globally over the years. Although of shorter duration, life expectancy has also increased in the developing countries and NCDs are expanding their share in populations' morbidity and mortality. If current trends of rise in obesity and overweight continue, it is expected that very soon NCDs, including diabetes, will become the main contributor to morbidity and mortality even in the poorest, low-income countries.

According to the recommendations from American Diabetes Association (ADA), screening for diabetes should begin at the age of 45 years at the latest, if no other risk factors are present [2]. Screening should be considered earlier in overweight or obese adults who have one or more additional risk factors for diabetes [2]. Those risk factors include prediabetes, GDM, first-degree relative with diabetes, high-risk race or ethnicity, history of cardiovascular disease (CVD), hypertension

© Springer Nature Switzerland AG 2021
I. Smokovski, *Managing Diabetes in Low Income Countries*,
https://doi.org/10.1007/978-3-030-51469-3_2

($\geq$140/90 mmHg or treatment for hypertension), HDL <0.90 mmol/L (35 mg/dL) or triglycerides >2.82 mmol/L (250 mg/dL), polycystic ovary syndrome, physical inactivity, severe obesity, or acanthosis nigricans [2]. If results are normal, testing for diabetes should be repeated at least every 3 years [2]. These recommendations have been widely adopted not only in developed, but also in developing countries.

Obesity is the most critical factor for developing insulin resistance and inadequate insulin secretion, leading to the development of prediabetes and diabetes. Prevalence of overweight and obesity is continuously rising worldwide.

Overweight is defined as BMI between 25 kg/m^2 and 30 kg/m^2, and obesity as BMI above 30 kg/m^2. In Asian populations the cut off values for overweight are lower, at 23 kg/m^2. Obesity is the main reason not only for the exponential rise of type 2 diabetes prevalence in adults, but also for the growing prevalence of type 2 diabetes in children and adolescents. Rising obesity prevalence in youth results in development of diabetes at an earlier age compared to previous generations.

Obesity and inadequate physical activity are important modifiable risk factors for the development of type 2 diabetes. One of the main goals of managing the burden of diabetes prevalence is to halt the rise in overweight and obesity [2, 3].

Recently, the WHO reported that worldwide obesity has nearly tripled since 1975 [4]. In 2016, more than 1.9 billion adults were overweight (prevalence of 39%), and of these over 650 million were obese (prevalence of 13%) [4]. Most of the world's population currently live in countries where overweight and obesity are associated with higher mortality compared to underweight. It has also been reported that over 340 million children and adolescents aged 5–19 were overweight or obese in 2016 [4].

Furthermore, the WHO reported that the number of overweight or obese infants and young children (aged 0–5 years) increased from 32 million globally in 1990 to 41 million in 2016 [5]. The vast majority of overweight or obese young children live in developing countries, where the increase has been more than 30% higher than of developed countries [5]. Without intervention, obese infants and young children will likely continue to be obese during childhood and adulthood [5].

Earlier studies reported high prevalence of childhood obesity (5–19 years) in developing countries: 41.8% in Mexico, 22.1% in Brazil, 22.0% in India, and 19.3% in Argentina [6]. Important factors contributing to the childhood obesity in developing countries included high socioeconomic status, residence in urban municipalities, female gender, unawareness about nutrition, marketing by global food companies, increased academic stress, and poor facilities for physical activity [6].

Recent reports have shown that almost 40% of adults and 18.5% of young people in the US are obese, and that only one quarter of youth meets the recommendations on physical activity [7]. It has been reported that incidence of type 2 diabetes among those aged 10 to 19 years in the US, increased from 9 per 100,000 in 2002–2003 to 13.8 per 100,000 in 2014–2015 [7]. In recent years, considerable increase of screen time has also been associated with reduced levels of physical activity and increase in obesity.

In a US study of the impact of obesity on mortality, it has been demonstrated that 1 in 5 fatal cases was associated with obesity, which was three times above the previous estimations [8]. It is paradoxical that convenient living, including increased calories intake and lower levels of physical activity results in alarming rates of obesity and is predicted to affect the life expectancy in the US. For the first time ever, it may occur that children in the US would live shorter compared to their parents, which is mainly due to the obesity related disorders.

Obesity rise is no longer exclusive for developed countries. It has become one of the main healthcare concerns in developing countries as well. Taking into account past and current BMI trends, it is anticipated that obesity will continue to rise in developing countries. In the coming years, the mean BMI in developed countries could be exceeded by developing countries [9, 10]. Rather than focusing on obesity at the individual level, activities need to be undertaken at the community and national level [9, 10].

Initially, the daily increase in calories intake per person and the rise of obesity were primarily related to parts of population with higher socioeconomic status among developing countries [9, 10]. However, recent trends demonstrate that rise in obesity is more prevalent in parts of populations with lower socioeconomic status in developing countries, which is in line with the similar observations in developed countries [9, 10]. The availability and low cost of fast foods contribute to those unfavorable trends.

Studies report that 70% of the fast-foods and almost half of the full-service restaurant meals eaten in the US were of poor nutritional value [9, 10]. Unfortunately, those dietary patterns are now replicated in developing countries due to the lower costs per calories intake. It has been reported that lower socioeconomic status, lower level of education, lower physical activity, and lower cost per calorie, are critical factors associated with the increase of BMI [9, 10].

It is tragic that in many countries, both developed and developing, there are parents who are sometimes more worried about whether they can afford their children or themselves any meal, and much less if the meal is healthy or not. Such situations are, understandably, more common in developing countries.

Rates of urbanization are increasing in the developing countries resulting in a sedentary lifestyle associated with lower levels of physical exercise and eating less healthy foods. With the wider adoption of industrialization and technology, labor intensive activities are decreasing in developing countries, contributing to the rise of obesity and associated diabetes.

As the overweight and obesity are becoming more prevalent in youth, ADA is recommending risk-based screening for type 2 diabetes or prediabetes in children and adolescents who are overweight (equal or greater than 85th percentile) or obese (equal or greater than 95th percentile), and who have one or more additional risk factors, such as maternal history of diabetes or GDM, family history of type 2 diabetes, high-risk race or ethnicity, signs of insulin resistance or conditions associated with insulin resistance (acanthosis nigricans, hypertension, dyslipidemia, polycystic ovary syndrome) [2].

Additional parameters closely related to visceral obesity, despite the widely used BMI, are waist circumference and waist-to-hip ratio. Obesity has been closely related to hypertension and dyslipidemia, major risk factors for CVDs. The rise in obesity is also associated with the increase of diabetes related cases of cancer world-wide [3].

Increased calories intake per person per day has been a strong driver for the increased diabetes prevalence in the Republic of North Macedonia. The rising diabetes prevalence could be explained by the similarity of the dietary pattern and lifestyle in the Republic of North Macedonia with those of the population in Turkey, a country with the highest diabetes prevalence in Europe [3, 11, 12]. This might be due to the fact that the Ottoman Empire had occupied the territory of the modern Republic of North Macedonia for more than five centuries until the beginning of the twentieth century, exerting a huge influence on the diet and lifestyle of the local population. Such a diet is mainly based on non-integral wheat flour, bread, pastry, lots of sweets, high-fat meals, and a lifestyle characterized by no, or inadequate physical activity [11, 12].

There has been a significant change in dietary patterns since the early 1990s, when the Republic of North Macedonia gained its independence from the former Yugoslavia. Total daily calories per person per day increased by almost 50% in the country in less than 20 years, since the beginning of 1990 [11]. It was paralleled with the rising rates of overweight (53% of the population) and obesity [11]. Prevalence of obesity in the population above 18 years has increased from 17.7% in 2000, to 21.9% in 2016 (Fig. 2.1) [13].

Given the importance of obesity as a diabetes driver, it would be necessary to monitor the individual values of BMI in the Electronic Healthcare Records (EHRs). By doing so, it would be possible to monitor the prevalence of obesity at a national

Fig. 2.1 Prevalence of adult obesity in the Republic of North Macedonia, data adapted from [13]

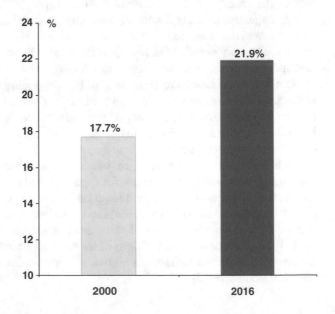

level. National e-Health System is critical for recording metabolic parameters and monitoring the prevalence of obesity in the country.

Ethnicities are well established to be associated with different diabetes prevalence. One example is the ethnicities in the US, such as African Americans, Hispano Americans, Native Americans, Asian Americans, and Pacific Islanders, who have higher diabetes prevalence than the Caucasians [14]. The rates of increase of type 2 diabetes in the younger population have also been higher among racial and ethnic minority groups compared to the Caucasians in the US [14].

Globally, populations with highest diabetes age-adjusted, comparative prevalence include Marshall Islands (30.5%), Kiribati (22.5%), Sudan (22.1%), Tuvalu (22.1%), Mauritius (22.0%), New Caledonia (21.8%), Pakistan (19.9%), French Polynesia (19.5%), Solomon Islands (19.0%), Guam (18.7%) [3]. These top 10 countries in terms of diabetes prevalence, except for the French and US colonies (New Caledonia, French Polynesia, Guam), are middle- or low-income countries.

There are multiple factors that contribute to the disparities among different ethnicities, including biological and genetic factors, socioeconomic status, and access to the healthcare system [14]. It is common that most minority populations are of lower socioeconomic status and have limited access to the healthcare system.

Ethnic differences could be illustrated by the facts that South Asians have lower age at onset of type 2 diabetes, lower BMI threshold for type 2 diabetes, more rapid decline in beta cell function, low muscle mass, increased abdominal obesity, and increased non-alcoholic fatty liver disease (NAFLD) prevalence, compared to Caucasians [15].

Higher diabetes prevalence in rural compared to urban population in the Republic of North Macedonia was also explained by the differences in respective ethnic populations. Namely, rural municipalities are mainly inhabited by ethnic Albanians who share dietary and lifestyle habits more closely to the Turkish population which has the highest diabetes prevalence in Europe, as compared to the ethnic Macedonian population mainly inhabiting the urban municipalities [12]. Therefore, developing countries should aim for ethnic stratification of diabetes prevalence due to the possible interethnic differences in diabetes pathophysiology.

Prediabetes, as a distinct medical condition, is another strong driver for the development of diabetes. Prediabetes is defined as FPG 5.6 mmol/L (100 mg/dL) to 6.9 mmol/L (125 mg/dL), i.e. Impaired Fasting Glucose (IFG); or 2-h PG during 75-g OGTT 7.8 mmol/L (140 mg/dL) to 11.0 mmol/L (199 mg/dL), i.e. Impaired Glucose Tolerance (IGT); or HbA1c 5.7–6.4% (39–47 mmol/mol) [2].

In addition to the steep rise of diabetes prevalence, there is a whole contingent of people just about to be diagnosed with diabetes, namely the people who are diagnosed with prediabetes. Management of prediabetes is of utmost importance, since diabetes prevention activities should primarily address the prediabetic population and could result in a delay of progression to diabetes, or even reverting to normoglycaemia.

It is estimated there were 374 million people with prediabetes (prevalence of 7.5%) in 2019 worldwide, at a very high risk for developing type 2 diabetes [3]. The estimated number of adults aged 20–79 years with prediabetes is predicted to rise to

454 million (prevalence of 8.0%) by 2030, and 548 million (prevalence of 8.6%) by 2045 [3].

Similar to the situation with diabetes prevalence, the vast majority of people with prediabetes come from developing countries. In 2019, 72.2% of adults with impaired glucose tolerance were living in low- and middle-income countries [3].

It was estimated that 269.9 million adults (20–79 years) with prediabetes were living in developing countries in 2019 (prevalence of 6.7%), compared to 104.1 million in developed countries (prevalence of 11.4%) (Fig. 2.2) [3]. The increase in prediabetes prevalence is expected to be faster in lower income countries, compared to higher income countries.

In 2030, it is estimated that 75% of the total number of adults with prediabetes will be coming from developing countries. Projections for 2030 is that 340.0 million people with prediabetes will be living in developing (prevalence of 7.2%), compared to 114.0 million in developed countries (prevalence of 12.1%) (Fig. 2.2) [3].

In 2045, it is estimated that 79% of the total number of adults with prediabetes will be coming from low- and middle-income countries. It is projected that 430.2 million adults with prediabetes will be living in developing (prevalence of 7.9%), compared to 117.8 million in developed countries (prevalence of 12.5%) (Fig. 2.2) [3].

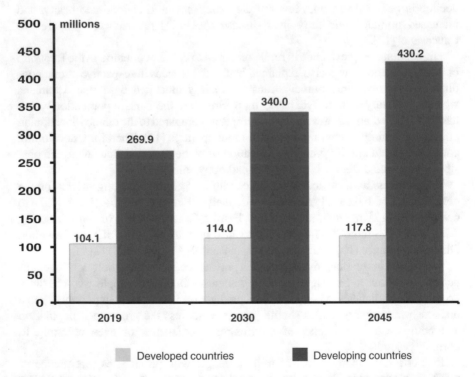

Fig. 2.2 Prediabetes prevalence in developed and developing countries, 2019–2045, data adapted from [3]

Prevalence of prediabetes is higher in the Republic of North Macedonia as a developing European country, compared to Europe as a region. Number of people in the age group 20–79 years with prediabetes in the Republic of North Macedonia was estimated at 120,700 in 2019, with age-adjusted comparative prevalence of prediabetes in this age group of 7.1%. It was considerably above the age-adjusted comparative prevalence of prediabetes in Europe, estimated at 4.4% [3].

For all the people with prediabetes, testing for diabetes should be conducted at least on a yearly basis [2]. It has been demonstrated from the Diabetes Prevention Program (DPP) studies that lifestyle interventions resulting in weight reduction were effective in delaying type 2 diabetes [16–31]. These studies suggest what needs to be done to delay or prevent prediabetes, if such lifestyle interventions are implemented in the normoglycaemic population.

It has to be emphasized that DPPs are complex and are not aimed only at high-risk, prediabetic population. Instead, those programs also include school teachers teaching pupils on nutrition and physical activity. In many cases, overweight and obese school teachers are trained to modify their lifestyle first, in order to convey the benefits of modified lifestyle to their pupils. Situation is similar with healthcare providers who need to be trained to improve their lifestyle before they could have an impact on the lifestyle of the people they are caring for.

People with prediabetes have to be monitored closely and should have the diagnosis of prediabetes recorded in their EHRs. In that way, the progression of prediabetes to diabetes could be followed at individual, but also at a national level. Activities to prevent diabetes should be addressing individuals with prediabetes and need to be regularly evaluated if effective.

Gestational diabetes is another critical risk factor for the development of type 2 diabetes. Screening for GDM is performed at 24–28 weeks of gestation in pregnant women not previously diagnosed with diabetes. Most commonly used criteria for diagnosis of GDM are meeting or exceeding any of the following PG values after OGTT: FPG 5.1 mmol/L (92 mg/dL), or 1 h-PG 10.0 mmol/L (180 mg/dL), or 2 h-PG 8.5 mmol/L (153 mg/dL) [2].

An estimated 15.8% (20.4 million) of live births were affected by hyperglycemia in pregnancy in 2019, and of those 83.6% were due to GDM [3]. The vast majority (86.8%) of cases of GDM come from low- and middle-income countries, where access to antenatal, perinatal and postnatal care has often been limited (Fig. 2.3) [3].

Prevalence of GDM increases rapidly with age, which is in reverse relation to the number of pregnancies that rapidly decreases with the age. As a result of the higher fertility rates in younger women, the absolute number of cases of GDM is higher in women under the age of 30 years [2, 3].

Gestational diabetes is associated with increased risk of type 2 diabetes in women later in their life. Women diagnosed with GDM have almost seven times higher risk of developing type 2 diabetes during their lifetime, compared to women with normoglycaemic pregnancy [32]. It has been reported that women with GDM have almost twice higher risk of developing CVD compared to women without GDM [33].

Gestational diabetes could result in an increased risk of childhood overweight and obesity, increased insulin resistance and higher risk of prediabetes in the

Fig. 2.3 Proportion of gestational diabetes in developed and developing countries, data adapted from [3]

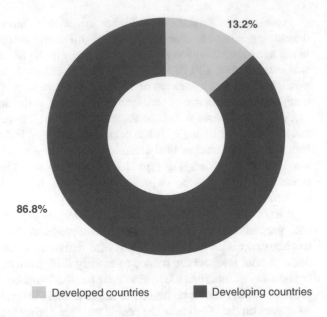

offspring [34]. Consequently, the offspring of a mother with GDM is at a higher risk of developing type 2 diabetes [34]. Women who were diagnosed with GDM should have lifelong testing for diabetes, at least every 3 years. Gestational diabetes has to be recorded in the individual EHRs, and to be followed at subsequent visits after delivery, to reassess the risk for developing type 2 diabetes.

Smoking is another very important risk factor for diabetes, especially in developing countries. This is important as in 2014, the US Surgeon General's Report identified for the first time that cigarette smoking not only raises the risk of vascular and other complications of diabetes, but it is a direct causative factor for type 2 diabetes [11, 35, 36]. The risk of developing diabetes is 30–40% higher for active smokers than non-smokers [35, 36].

The WHO estimates that tobacco is the largest cause of preventable mortality in the world. In 2015, it was estimated there were more than 933 million smokers worldwide. Smoking is responsible for almost six million deaths each year, or the loss of 140 million years of healthy life. Nearly 80% of the smokers, most of them males, are coming from the developing countries, a greater burden than malaria and HIV combined [37, 38].

Smoking is responsible for 5–6% of all morbidity globally and its share is rising over time [37, 38]. Tobacco use is increasing in developing countries and if no action is taken, the number of annual tobacco deaths is projected to rise to more than eight million by 2030, amounting to the loss of more than 200 million years of healthy life [37, 38].

Studies have confirmed that insulin is less effective in people with type 2 diabetes exposed to high levels of nicotine [11, 35]. Hence, those who smoke need larger doses of insulin to control their glycaemia. Furthermore, smokers who have diabetes are more likely to develop macro- and microvascular diabetes complica tions. Unfortunately, the Republic of North Macedonia is one of the top 10 countries of the world in smoking prevalence, which may also be the reason for the very high diabetes prevalence in the country [11].

As smoking is a major risk factor for CVD and diabetes, it is critical to know the smoking status of each individual. For that purpose, smoking status has to be recorded with the other metabolic parameters in individual EHRs, and should be monitored at subsequent visits. Monitoring of smoking prevalence at a national level would guide the authorities on the further steps to be taken, and to evaluate if previous anti-smoking policies were effective.

Psychosocial stress could also be considered as a strong, still not adequately recognized driver for the development of diabetes. Although suggested that emo tional stress might result in diabetes almost four centuries ago, it has just recently been reported that the majority of the effects of psychosocial stress on diabetes risk are not mediated through the traditional risk factors, such as hypertension, physical inactivity, smoking, inadequate diet, and obesity [39, 40]. Studies suggest that not only chronic stress, but also general emotional stress, anxiety, sleeping problems, anger, and hostility are associated with an increased risk for the development of type 2 diabetes [39, 40].

Population in developing countries is exposed to psychosocial stress to a higher extent compared to the developed countries, due to the higher levels of poverty, unemployment, unstable housing and limited food access in some cases. We can again take the Republic of North Macedonia as an example, with a sharp growth in prevalence of type 2 diabetes, especially after 1990 [11]. The strong contributor might have been the societal transition from a centrally planned economy guaran teeing jobs and income before 1990, to a market economy with job and income insecurity afterwards [11]. The, so called, 'transitional economy', has led to an unprecedented rise in unemployment and associated psychosocial stress, especially among the middle-aged population, which has largely contributed to the increase of diabetes prevalence in the country [11].

Medications, such as glucocorticoids, some HIV medications, and antipsychot ics [2, 41], are known to increase the risk of diabetes and should be considered when deciding if the individuals who are treated should be screened for diabetes. Cystic fibrosis and post-transplantation use of immunosuppressive medication are other rare factors for the development of diabetes [2].

The assessment of risk factors or use of a risk assessment tool is recommended to guide healthcare providers on whether to perform a screening test for diabetes. One of such risk assessment tools that could be used in developing countries is the ADA diabetes risk test [2]. This diabetes risk test is based on age, gender, history of GDM, family history of diabetes, history of hypertension, physical activity and weight.

Another risk score test used for type 2 diabetes is the FINDRISC (Finnish Diabetes Screening Risk) externally validated in numerous populations with accept able sensitivity and specificity. Diabetes risk with FINDRISC test is calculated based on the gender, age, BMI, use of blood pressure medications, history of high blood glucose, level of physical activity, daily consumption of vegetables, fruits or berries, and family history of diabetes [42].

The use of diabetes risk test might be of help to the providers to identify higher risk individuals for further investigations. Diabetes risk could also be recorded in the EHRs for further monitoring. If the NeHS is in place, the monitoring of diabetes drivers should be done at each physician's visit and could easily be implemented in a setting with limited resources.

What should be done to manage the diabetes drivers in developing countries?
Each developing country should …

- … set a national targets for curbing obesity, critical driver for diabetes prevalence;
- … target prediabetic population with dietary changes and increased physical activity;
- … screen every pregnant women for GDM due to considerably higher risk for type 2 diabetes for the mother and the offspring;
- … have comprehensive national policies for drastically reducing smoking prevalence;
- … enable that NeHS is used for monitoring of the diabetes drivers.

References

1. World Health Organization. World health statistics overview 2019: monitoring health for the SDGs, sustainable development goals. Geneva: World Health Organization; 2019.
2. American Diabetes Association. Standards of medical care in diabetes 2020. Diabetes Care. 2020;43(1):s1–212.
3. International Diabetes Federation. IDF Diabetes Atlas. 9th ed. Brussels: International Diabetes Federation; 2019.
4. World Health Organization. Obesity and Overweight. Facts and figures. https://www.who.int/en/news-room/fact-sheets/detail/obesity-and-overweight. Accessed 30 March 2020.
5. World Health Organization. Commission on Ending Childhood Obesity. Facts and figures on childhood obesity. https://www.who.int/end-childhood-obesity/facts/en/; Accessed 30 March 2020.
6. Gupta N, Goel K, Shah P, Misra A. Childhood obesity in developing countries: epidemiology, determinants, and prevention. Endocr Rev. 2012;33(1):48–70.
7. Centers for Disease Control and Prevention. Divers J, Mayer-Davis JE2, Lawrence MJ, Isom S, Dabelea D, Dolan L, Imperatore G, Marcovina S, Pettitt JD, Pihoker C, Hamman FR, Saydah S, Wagenknecht E. Trends in incidence of type 1 and type 2 diabetes among youths – selected counties and Indian reservations, United States, 2002–2015. MMWR, 2020; 69(6):161–165.
8. Ryan K, et al. The impact of obesity on US mortality levels: the importance of age and cohort factors in population estimates. Am J Public Health. 2013; https://doi.org/10.2105/AJPH.2013.301379.

9. Popkin MB, Adair SL, Ng WS. Global nutrition transition and the pandemic of obesity in developing countries. Nutr Rev. 2011;70(1):3–21.
10. Bhurosy T, Jeewon R. Overweight and obesity epidemic in developing countries: a problem with diet, physical activity, or socioeconomic status? The Scientific World Journal. 2014;2014:964236. doi: https://doi.org/10.1155/2014/964236.
11. Smokovski I, Milenkovic T, Trapp C, Mitov A. Diabetes care in the Republic of Macedonia: challenges and opportunities. Ann Global Health. 2015;81(6):792–802.
12. Smokovski I, Milenkovic T, Cho HN. First stratified diabetes prevalence data for Republic of Macedonia derived from the National eHealth System. Diabetes Res Clin Pract. 2018;143:179–83.
13. Food and Agriculture Organization of the United Nations. FAOStat, North Macedonia. http://www.fao.org/faostat/en/?#country/154. Accessed 12 April 2020.
14. Spanakis EK, Golden SH. Race/ethnic difference in diabetes and diabetic complications. Curr Diab Rep. 2013;13(6):814–23. https://doi.org/10.1007/s11892-013-0421-9.
15. Misra A, Gopalan H, Jayawardena R, Hills PA, Soares M, Reza-Albarrán AA, Ramaiya LK. Diabetes in developing countries. J Diabetes. 2019;11(7):522–39. https://doi.org/10.1111/1753-0407.12913.
16. Pan XR, Li GW, Hu YH, Wang JX, Yang WY, An ZX, et al. Effects of diet and exercise in preventing NIDDM in people with impaired glucose tolerance. The Da Qing IGT and Diabetes Study. Diabetes Care. 1997;20(4):537–44.
17. Li G, Zhang P, Wang J, An Y, Gong Q, Gregg EW, et al. Cardiovascular mortality, all-cause mortality, and diabetes incidence after lifestyle intervention for people with impaired glucose tolerance in the Da Qing Diabetes Prevention Study: a 23-year follow-up study. Lancet Diabetes Endocrinol. 2014;2(6):474–80.
18. Li G, Zhang P, Wang J, Gregg EW, Yang W, Gong Q, et al. The long-term effect of lifestyle interventions to prevent diabetes in the China Da Qing Diabetes Prevention Study: a 20-year follow-up study. Lancet. 2008;371(9626):1783–9.
19. Diabetes Prevention Program Research Group, Knowler WC, Fowler SE, Hamman RF, Christophi CA, Hoffman HJ, et al. 10-year follow-up of diabetes incidence and weight loss in the Diabetes Prevention Program Outcomes Study. Lancet. 2009;374(9702):1677–86.
20. Lindström J, Peltonen M, Eriksson JG, Ilanne-Parikka P, Aunola S, Keinänen-Kiukaanniemi S, et al. Improved lifestyle and decreased diabetes risk over 13 years: long-term follow-up of the randomised Finnish Diabetes Prevention Study (DPS). Diabetologia. 2013;56(2):284–93.
21. Nanditha A, Snehalatha C, Raghavan A, Vinitha R, Satheesh K, Susairaj P, et al. The post-trial analysis of the Indian SMS diabetes prevention study shows persistent beneficial effects of lifestyle intervention. Diabetes Res Clin Pract. 2018;142:213–21.
22. Herman WH, Hoerger TJ, Brandle M, Hicks K, Sorensen S, Zhang P, et al. The cost-effectiveness of lifestyle modification or metformin in preventing type 2 diabetes in adults with impaired glucose tolerance. Ann Intern Med. 2005;142(5):323–32.
23. Tuomilehto J, Lindström J, Eriksson JG, Valle TT, Hämäläinen H, Ilanne-Parikka P, et al. Prevention of type 2 diabetes mellitus by changes in lifestyle among subjects with impaired glucose tolerance. N Engl J Med. 2001;344(18):1343–50.
24. Knowler WC, Barrett-Connor E, Fowler SE, Hamman RF, Lachin JM, Walker EA, et al. Reduction in the incidence of type 2 diabetes with lifestyle intervention or metformin. N Engl J Med. 2002;346(6):393–403.
25. Ramachandran A, Snehalatha C, Mary S, Mukesh B, Bhaskar AD, Vijay V, et al. The Indian Diabetes Prevention Programme shows that lifestyle modification and metformin prevent type 2 diabetes in Asian Indian subjects with impaired glucose tolerance (IDPP-1). Diabetologia. 2006;49(2):289–97.
26. Ramachandran A, Snehalatha C, Mary S, Selvam S, Kumar CKS, Seeli AC, et al. Pioglitazone does not enhance the effectiveness of lifestyle modification in preventing conversion of impaired glucose tolerance to diabetes in Asian Indians: results of the Indian Diabetes Prevention Programme-2 (IDPP-2). Diabetologia. 2009;52(6):1019–26.

27. Ramachandran A, Snehalatha C, Ram J, Selvam S, Simon M, Nanditha A, et al. Effectiveness of mobile phone messaging in prevention of type 2 diabetes by lifestyle modification in men in India: a prospective, parallel-group, randomised controlled trial. Lancet Diabetes Endocrinol. 2013;1(3):191–8.
28. Weber MB, Ranjani H, Staimez LR, Anjana RM, Ali MK, Narayan KMV, et al. The stepwise approach to diabetes prevention: results from the D-CLIP Randomized Controlled Trial. Diabetes Care. 2016;39(10):1760–7.
29. Iqbal Hydrie MZ, Basit A, Shera AS, Hussain A. Effect of intervention in subjects with high risk of diabetes mellitus in Pakistan. J Nutr Metab. 2012;2012:867604. https://doi.org/10.1155/2012/867604.
30. Kosaka K, Noda M, Kuzuya T. Prevention of type 2 diabetes by lifestyle intervention: a Japanese trial in IGT males. Diabetes Res Clin Pract. 2005;67(2):152–62.
31. Saito T, Watanabe M, Nishida J, Izumi T, Omura M, Takagi T, et al. Lifestyle modification and prevention of type 2 diabetes in overweight Japanese with impaired fasting glucose levels: a randomized controlled trial. Arch Intern Med. 2011;171(15):1352–60.
32. Bellamy L, Casas J-P, Hingorani AD, Williams D. Type 2 diabetes mellitus after gestational diabetes: a systematic review and meta-analysis. Lancet. 2009;373(9677):1773–9.
33. Li J, Song C, Li C, Liu P, Sun Z, Yang X. Increased risk of cardiovascular disease in women with prior gestational diabetes: a systematic review and meta-analysis. Diabetes Res Clin Pract. 2018;140:324–38.
34. Lowe WL, Scholtens DM, Kuang A, Linder B, Lawrence JM, Lebenthal Y, et al. Hyperglycemia and adverse pregnancy outcome follow-up study (HAPO FUS): maternal gestational diabetes mellitus and childhood glucose metabolism. Diabetes Care. 2019;42(3):372–80.
35. U.S. Department of Health and Human Services. The Health Consequences of Smoking: 50 Years of Progress. A Report of the Surgeon General. Atlanta, GA: U.S. Department of Health and Human Services, Centers for Disease Control and Prevention, National Center for Chronic Disease Prevention and Health Promotion, Office on Smoking and Health, 2014.
36. Ng M, Freeman KM, Fleming DT, et al. Smoking prevalence and cigarette consumption in 187 countries, 1980-2012. JAMA. 2014;311:183e92.
37. World Health Organization. Tobacco. Facts and figures. https://www.who.int/news-room/fact-sheets/detail/tobacco. Accessed 30 March 2020.
38. Prabhat J, et al. 21st-century hazards of smoking and benefits of cessation in the United States. N Engl J Med. 2014;368(4):341–50.
39. Harris LM, Oldmeadow C, Hure A, Luu J, Loxton D, Attia J. Stress increases the risk of type 2 diabetes onset in women: a 12-year longitudinal study using causal modelling. PLoS One. 2017;12(2):e0172126. https://doi.org/10.1371/journal.pone.0172126.
40. Pouwer F, Kupper N, Adriaanse CM, et al. Does emotional stress cause type 2 diabetes mellitus? A review from the European Depression in Diabetes (EDID) Research Consortium. Discov Med. 2010;9(45):112–8.
41. Erickson SC, Le L, Zakharyan A, et al. New-onset treatment-dependent diabetes mellitus and hyperlipidemia associated with atypical antipsychotic use in older adults without schizophrenia or bipolar disorder. J Am Geriatr Soc. 2012;60:474–9.
42. Meijnikman AS, De Block CEM, Verrijken A, et al. Predicting type 2 diabetes mellitus: a comparison between the FINDRISC score and the metabolic syndrome. Diabetol Metab Syndr. 2018;10:12. https://doi.org/10.1186/s13098-018-0310-0.

Chapter 3
Impact of Diabetes Complications

Diabetes complications are generally divided into **acute complications**, including diabetic ketoacidosis (DKA), hyperglycaemic hyperosmolar state (HHS) and hypoglycemia; and **chronic complications**, including macrovascular and microvascular complications.

Diabetic ketoacidosis is the initial clinical manifestation in many cases of type 1 diabetes. According to the recent IDF estimates, there were 128,900 newly diagnosed cases of type 1 diabetes in 2019 globally [1]. The increase in incidence of type 1 diabetes results in higher number of cases of DKA.

Initial clinical presentation as DKA is found in 25% of cases with type 1 diabetes in developed countries, such as the UK, France, Poland, and the US [1–5]. The high incidence of this life-threatening diabetes complication urged launch of campaigns for increasing public awareness of type 1 diabetes, and earlier diagnosis among children and adolescents [1, 6].

Situation in countries with limited resources is worse as new onset type 1 diabetes is often misdiagnosed, resulting in higher incidence of DKA as initial presentation [1]. It has been reported that 75% of all endocrine pediatric emergencies in developing countries are children with type 1 diabetes and DKA [7].

Diabetic ketoacidosis is a major cause of mortality in children with type 1 diabetes in developing countries. Unfortunately, there are striking differences between developed and developing countries in terms of DKA related mortality. Rates of mortality caused by DKA in developing countries are in the range of 6–24% compared to 0.15–0.31% in developed countries (Fig. 3.1) [7–9]. It is alarming that the relative risk of DKA related mortality in developing countries is up to 40–80 times higher than in developed countries.

Hyperglycaemic hyperosmolar state (HHS) in developing countries was associated with newly diagnosed type 2 diabetes and poor glycaemic control due to non-adherence to prescribed diabetes medications [10]. There are limited data on hypoglycemia in developing countries; however, it is reported to be associated with significantly increased risk of mortality [11].

© Springer Nature Switzerland AG 2021   25
I. Smokovski, *Managing Diabetes in Low Income Countries*,
https://doi.org/10.1007/978-3-030-51469-3_3

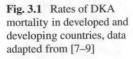 **Fig. 3.1** Rates of DKA mortality in developed and developing countries, data adapted from [7–9]

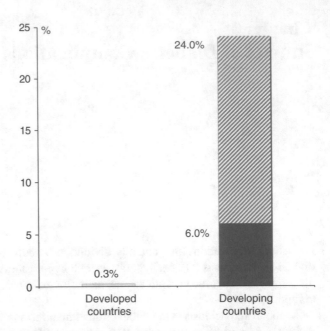

Chronic diabetes complications are generally divided into **macrovascular** and **microvascular**. Macrovascular complications include coronary artery disease, congestive heart failure, cerebrovascular disease and peripheral vascular disease. Many people with diabetes suffer from silent myocardial ischemia and sudden cardiac death [12]. Microvascular complications include retinopathy, nephropathy and neuropathy.

Additionally, diabetes has been reported as a major risk factor for increased morbidity and mortality in those infected in the recent pandemic of COVID-19. The increased morbidity and mortality have been particularly relevant for the people with diabetes complications. One of the possible explanations for the worse outcomes of COVID-19 in people with diabetes could be the effects of hyperglycemia on the suppression of the immune system, as those with inadequate glycaemic control have increased risk for any infection. It is due to the hyperglycemia and diabetes complications that people with diabetes have been categorized as very high risk for the COVID-19 related morbidity and mortality. On the other hand, contracting COVID-19 by people with diabetes increases their risk of developing acute diabetes complications.

It has recently been reported that people with diabetes and COVID-19 were more likely to suffer from severe pneumonia, excessive inflammation responses and hypercoagulable state, compared with those who had COVID-19 but not diabetes [13]. Another recent study found that while diabetes does not increase the likelihood of being infected with COVID-19, those with diabetes may experience worse outcomes from the disease, including death [14]. Based on the data from 12 studies about the prevalence of diabetes among adults with COVID-19, findings were in line with the association between diabetes and excess mortality from any acute and chronic condition, including infections [14].

Cardiovascular diseases are the main cause of mortality worldwide, exceeding all the other causes. It is estimated that approximately 18 million people have died from CVDs in 2016, representing one third of the total mortality worldwide. The largest share of cardiovascular deaths (85%) is due to coronary artery and cerebrovascular disease [15].

It was mentioned that approximately 4.2 million adults aged 20–79 years have died due to diabetes and its complications in 2019, representing 11.3% of the global mortality from all causes in this age group [1]. Sadly, almost half of the diabetes related mortality was in people under the age of 60 years [1].

Cardiovascular diseases are the leading cause of morbidity and mortality in people with diabetes. Development of CVDs in people with insulin resistance, the main underlying disorder in type 2 diabetes, is a progressive and long-term process, characterized by endothelial dysfunction and vascular inflammation leading to formation of atherosclerotic plaques. It is estimated that 80% of people with type 2 diabetes would die from cardiovascular events [1, 16, 17].

People with diabetes have two to four times higher risk of developing CVD compared to non-diabetes population. The relative risk is higher in people with diabetes of younger age and in women [1, 17, 18]. Diabetes related mortality is higher in women than in men (2.3 million vs 1.9 million, respectively), and this excess risk can be mainly attributed to the higher risk of cardiovascular mortality in women with diabetes [1, 19]. Increased risk for CVD begins in the pre-diabetic range as the current cut-off values for diagnosis of diabetes are defined according to the increased risk for microvascular complications, such as retinopathy.

Most common form of CVD in people with diabetes, as in the general population, is coronary artery disease [20]. Recent study estimated the prevalence of CVD in people with type 2 diabetes at 32.2%, and majority of those were diagnosed with coronary artery disease (21.2%) (Fig. 3.2) [20].

Fig. 3.2 Prevalence of CVD and coronary artery disease in people with type 2 diabetes, data adapted from [20]

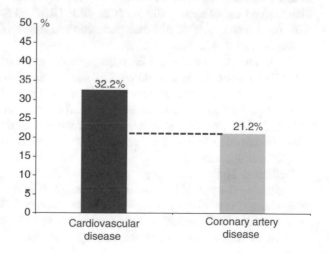

The incidence of CVD and the associated mortality has declined in developed countries in the recent decades. The efforts of many developed countries to reduce the major cardiovascular risk factors, such as dyslipidemia, hypertension and smoking, resulted in a progressive reduction of cardiovascular morbidity and mortality in these countries [1, 15]. It is only obesity and the associated diabetes that manifest a trend of continued growth, and if such trends are not reversed, they have the potential to overcome the positive effects of the reduction of other major cardiovascular risk factors [1, 15].

However, those trends of reduced CVD morbidity and mortality have not been replicated in developing countries [1, 15]. The burden of CVDs is enormous in developing countries as 75% of all cardiovascular deaths occur in those countries [15]. People with diabetes in developing countries have a higher prevalence of CVD compared to developed countries [1, 20]. Possible explanations could be the higher prevalence of the major risk factors, such as smoking, uncontrolled hypertension and uncontrolled dyslipidemia. Psychosocial stress and lower levels of physical activity also play a role in the development of CVD.

The management of CVDs in developing countries is complex since they often lack fully functioning healthcare systems able to timely diagnose and treat those affected at an early stage. Furthermore, people from developing countries are lacking modern treatment options, including medications and technology, which is the reason the cardiovascular mortality rates are higher in middle- and low-income countries [20, 21]. Epidemiological studies including people of South Asian origin have shown a 2–3 times higher risk of developing CVD compared to Caucasians [20, 21].

Taking into consideration the magnitude of the problem, CVDs exert a huge burden not only on the healthcare systems, but on the whole societies and economies, especially of developing countries. People with diabetes related CVD in developing countries are covering many of the healthcare expenditures 'out of pocket', which might be a challenge for the timely and adequate management. Latest diabetes treatments for reduction of cardiovascular outcomes in people with diabetes and established CVD, such as GLP-1RA and SGLT2i, remain available only for a minor part of diabetes population in developing countries, or are not available at all due to their cost.

Cardiovascular diseases are the most prevalent cause of morbidity and mortality in the Republic of North Macedonia [22]. It is estimated that almost two thirds of all cases of morbidity in the country are due to CVD [22]. The country has recently been categorized as a very high risk European country for cardiovascular mortality [22, 23]. High diabetes prevalence and strong association between diabetes and CVD, further contribute to the complexity of diabetes burden on the socioeconomic prospects of the country.

Dedicated National Program on CVDs has been introduced in the country strengthening the public healthcare resources, such as opening of novel centers for interventional cardiology aiming to have one center per 200,000 inhabitants, introduction of neonatal cardiac surgery, opening of adult University Clinic of Cardiac Surgery, as previously all cardiac surgery interventions were performed in the private clinics. In addition, a lot has been invested in the education of physicians and nurses in the areas of cardiology and cardiac surgery, and the introduction of novel methods was strongly encouraged.

Since most of the cardiovascular risk factors are modifiable, and CVDs are the major cause of morbidity and mortality in developing countries, there is a huge opportunity to curb the increasing trends of CVD prevalence in a setting with limited resources. Preventive activities should include control of hypertension, dyslipidemia and hyperglycemia, increasing physical activity, reduction of obesity, termination of smoking, and management of psychosocial stress.

Diabetic retinopathy is a microvascular complication considered to be the leading cause of blindness in the population of working age globally [1]. Blindness caused by diabetic retinopathy has devastating consequences, not only for the person with diabetes, but for the whole society. If diagnosed early, diabetic retinopathy in many cases could be treated to prevent further worsening and development of blindness. In addition to diabetic retinopathy, macular edema, cataracts and glaucoma are also more prevalent in people with diabetes [1].

It is reported that almost one third of all people with diabetes have some form of diabetic retinopathy, and one third of them have the most severe, vision threatening form of diabetic retinopathy [1]. Diabetic retinopathy has been associated with inadequate glycaemic control, duration of diabetes, and with some major cardiovascular factors, such as hypertension and smoking [1].

Healthcare systems in developing countries that do not include routine screening for diabetic retinopathy have to face the burden of people with diabetes developing proliferative retinopathy or diabetic maculopathy, and ultimately blindness, taking a huge toll on the limited resources. The burden of diabetic retinopathy in developing countries is highest, and the readiness of healthcare systems to manage it is lowest.

Diabetic retinopathy has been strongly associated with type 1 diabetes [1]. In people with type 2 diabetes, the prevalence of diabetic retinopathy is higher in developing countries [1]. It is reported that the annual incidence of diabetic retinopathy ranges from 2.2% to 12.7%, and annual progression to sight threatening diabetic retinopathy ranges from 3.4% to 12.3% [24].

Evidence from the developed healthcare systems confirm that systematic screening for diabetic retinopathy results in reduction of incidence of visual impairment and blindness [25, 26]. Innovative approaches are required for the management of diabetes retinopathy in healthcare systems with limited resources and minimal infrastructure. Lack of qualified and competent resources in developing countries could often be substituted by the use of modern technology, especially with the recent introduction of diabetic retinopathy cameras with integrated artificial intelligence [27]. Those technologies could facilitate detection of cases where early treatment is needed to prevent further deterioration. They could also enable remote analysis of captured images by qualified and competent healthcare providers [27].

According to the WHO World Report on Vision, 146 million people had diabetic retinopathy, and 45 million had vision threatening diabetic retinopathy in 2019 [28].

By 2040, it is anticipated that 70 million people will have vision threatening diabetic retinopathy (Fig. 3.3) [28].

The WHO recognizes diabetic retinopathy as one of the five most common causes of moderate and severe visual impairment and blindness that is preventable and treatable. Although the target set by WHO was to reduce prevalence of avoidable visual impairment by 25% by 2019, this target has not been achieved in the developing countries [28].

Diabetic nephropathy, a form of Chronic Kidney Disease (CKD), is a microvascular diabetes complication and a leading cause for end stage renal disease. It is estimated that 38% of people with type 2 diabetes will develop CKD, and half of them will develop moderate to severe CKD (Fig. 3.4) [29, 30].

Fig. 3.3 Number of people with vision threatening diabetic retinopathy, data adapted from [28]

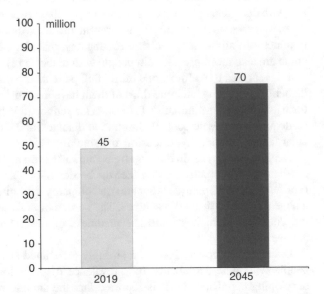

Fig. 3.4 Prevalence of CKD in people with type 2 diabetes, data adapted from [29, 30]

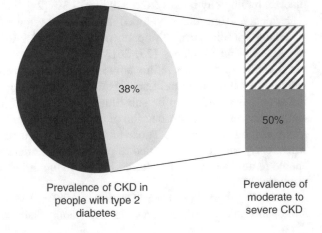

Globally, 80% of all cases of end stage renal disease requiring dialysis are caused by diabetes, hypertension or combination of both [1]. The prevalence of end stage renal disease in diabetes population is ten times higher compared to non-diabetes population [1]. There has been a continuous rise in CKD, mainly associated with the rising prevalence of type 2 diabetes. End stage renal disease and dialysis is another huge challenge for the healthcare systems, especially in developing countries [1].

In order to reduce the burden of diabetic nephropathy, early diagnosis and treatment of CKD is mandatory. Routine screening for albuminuria, Urinary Albumin Creatinine Ratio (UACR), and calculation of estimated Glomerular Filtration Rate (eGFR) is a simple and cost-effective strategy to identify those at risk, and initiate a timely treatment, even in a setting with limited resources [31]. There is a strong association between CKD and other macrovascular and microvascular complications. Major cardiovascular risk factors play significant role in the development and progression of CKD.

Financial burden of diabetic nephropathy is enormous, even in the healthcare systems of developed countries. In the US, it is estimated that mean annual healthcare costs were almost 50% higher among people with diabetic nephropathy compared to people with diabetes without nephropathy [1, 32]. People with diabetes undergoing dialysis have 300% higher annual healthcare costs compared to people with type 2 diabetes without complications, and those with end stage renal disease and kidney transplantation have 500% higher costs [1, 32].

People with diabetes and **peripheral vascular disease** (PVD) have an increased risk of diabetic foot amputation, coronary artery disease, cerebrovascular disease, and increased risk of mortality [1, 33, 34]. Routine screening of PVD is mandatory as approximately half of the people with diabetes and PVD are asymptomatic, and one third have atypical symptoms [1, 35–37].

Diabetic neuropathy is very prevalent in people with diabetes; it is estimated that up to 87% experience some form of diabetic neuropathy, and one quarter of them suffer from painful diabetic neuropathy [38]. It is strongly associated with diabetic foot complications and PVD.

A systematic review has reported an increase of 23.5% in the decade between 2000 and 2010 in the number of people living with PVD, and it is the most common initial manifestation of CVD in people with type 2 diabetes [39, 40].

The outcome of individuals with PVD depends on the comorbidities, advanced age, smoking and glycaemic control [41]. Inadequate control of metabolic parameters was associated with a greater need for lower extremity bypass surgery and amputation, and worse outcomes following vascular surgery [42].

People with diabetes have 10 to 20 times higher risk for lower limb amputation compared to people without diabetes [43]. It has been estimated that one amputation of the lower limb as a complication of diabetes occurs every 30 s globally [44].

Diabetic foot ulcers and amputations are more common in low- and middle-income countries than in high-income countries [45]. The prevalence of diabetic foot ulcers is higher among people with type 2 diabetes compared with those with type 1 diabetes [46]. People with diabetes who have foot ulcers have health expenditures five times higher than those without foot ulcers [1, 47].

Examination of the feet of people with diabetes and evaluation of circulation in lower extremities, in addition to education on self-inspection of feet, provides a cost-effective strategy for early diagnosis and treatment of PVD in a setting with limited resources.

Diabetes and related complications are exerting a huge **economic impact** on the healthcare systems and national economies. Total diabetes costs are composed of direct and indirect costs. Direct costs of diabetes include all diabetes related health-care expenditures from both public and private sources [1, 48]. The indirect costs of diabetes include loss of production resulting from disability, mortality, absenteeism (absence from work), and presenteeism (reduced productivity when at work) [1, 49].

Historically, direct diabetes costs have been continuously rising, from USD 232 billion worldwide in 2007, to USD 727 billion in 2017, and USD 760 billion in 2019, for the age group 20–79 years. The trend of rising costs is expected to continue to reach USD 825 billion by 2030, and USD 845 billion by 2045 [1].

Diabetes treatment is a small portion of the healthcare budget allocated for diabetes in developed countries, at a level of approximately 10%. Majority of the diabetes related direct costs in developed countries are due to diabetes complications and resulting hospitalizations [1, 50].

Situation is different in the developing countries where diabetes treatment takes a higher portion of the healthcare budget. The example of the Republic of North Macedonia was already mentioned with the tremendous cost of insulin and related supplies at the level of 40% of the budget allocated for all reimbursed, non-hospital medications (Fig. 1.4) [22, 51].

Furthermore, approximately 20% of the total healthcare budgets in South and Central American countries and 15% in Middle East and North African countries are allocated for diabetes, compared to 8.3% in Europe [1].

Although screening of early diagnosis of diabetes complications is associated with certain healthcare costs, their late diagnosis and treatment results in even higher costs, largely contributing to the overall economic impact.

These significant economic effects of diabetes complications on direct costs have been reported from the developed countries, such as Germany, the UK, the US and Italy [1, 52–59]. Studies of the economic impact of diabetes in developing countries also indicate a large economic burden [60]. Healthcare expenditures for diabetes and its adverse effects on the labor market are expected to increase over time and with disease severity, indicating that early investments into prevention and disease management may be particularly cost-effective in countries with limited resources [60].

Treatment of diabetes complications is a major driver of direct costs, and the main complications identified include: CVDs, diabetes foot complications, including amputations, diabetic retinopathy, and diabetic nephropathy. Direct costs are clearly related to the number of complications present, with mean annual healthcare expenditures for people with four or more complications being 20 times higher than in people with diabetes without complications [1, 52–59].

Control of major risk factors in people with type 2 diabetes can be cost-effective strategy in reducing CVDs. Screening for diabetic retinopathy is very cost-effective compared with no screening; and comprehensive foot care reduces costs by preventing ulcers and amputations in high-risk people with diabetes [61]. Improved care and subsequent prevention of complications results not only in better healthcare outcomes, but is also highly cost-effective [61].

The highest overall diabetes-related costs on a country level were estimated for the US with USD 294.6 billion, followed by China and Brazil, with USD 109.0 billion and USD 52.3 billion, respectively [1]. The countries with the lowest diabetes-related costs are lower resource countries, such as Sao Tome and Principe, and Tuvalu, with estimates of USD 1.1 million and USD 1.8 million [1].

There is a huge difference if we compare the countries according to the diabetes related expenditures per person in 2019. Countries with the highest annual expenditure per person are Switzerland with USD 11,916, followed by the US and Norway with USD 9,506 and USD 9,061; respectively [1]. Countries with the lowest annual expenditure per person are Bangladesh (USD 64), Central African Republic (USD 72) and Nepal (USD 80) [1]. Understandably, lower resource countries are spending less for diabetes per person, which affects the quality of care and increases the risk for even more costly diabetes complications.

It is worth mentioning that indirect costs add up to the overall diabetes burden, and need to be taken into consideration when evaluating the cost-effectiveness of diabetes care. Latest estimates suggest that indirect costs contribute with close to 35% of total diabetes costs, calculated at USD 1.31 trillion in 2015 [1, 62].

In high-income countries indirect costs were estimated at a level of 36.5%, compared to 31.7% in middle-income and 37.8% in low-income countries. Although there is a small difference between these groupings in terms of the share of the indirect costs, there is a considerable variation in the structure of the indirect costs [1, 62].

Disability and mortality are dominant in the global figures for indirect costs with 48.5% and 45.5%, respectively. Situation with structure of indirect costs is similar in high-income countries (59.2% and 35.5%). However, mortality contributes with 63.6% of indirect costs in middle-income countries, and 90.6% in low-income countries. Absenteeism and presenteeism together contribute 6% globally and less than 3% in low-income countries [1, 62].

It is important to estimate the economic impact of undiagnosed diabetes on the healthcare costs, since it could result in diagnosing diabetes complications at an advanced stage which is associated with higher costs.

Diabetes complications, due to their enormous impact on both direct and indirect costs, have to be included in the National Diabetes Plan. Efforts should be made by each developing country to estimate the prevalence of diabetes complications. Procedures for screening diabetes complications have to be included in the National Diabetes Care guidelines.

Frequent screening for diabetes complications results in early diagnosis and treatment that is a cost-effective compared to their treatment at a more advanced stage. Meticulous screening is particularly valuable under the conditions with limited resources.

What should be done to manage the impact of diabetes complications?
Each developing country should …

- … evaluate the prevalence of diabetes complications;
- … implement mandatory screening for CVD, retinopathy, nephropathy, PVD, as stipulated in the National Diabetes Care guidelines;
- … define screening frequency for diabetes complications;
- … determine the total cost, including direct and indirect costs;
- … empower National Diabetes Committee to monitor adherence to National Diabetes Care guidelines related to the screening of diabetes complications.

References

1. International Diabetes Federation. IDF Diabetes Atlas. 9th ed. Brussels: International Diabetes Federation; 2019.
2. Lansdown AJ, Barton J, Warner J, Williams D, Gregory JW, Harvey JN, et al. Prevalence of ketoacidosis at diagnosis of childhood onset Type 1 diabetes in Wales from 1991 to 2009 and effect of a publicity campaign. Diabet Med. 2012;29(12):1506–9.
3. Choleau C, Maitre J, Elie C, Barat P, Bertrand AM, de Kerdanet M, et al. Ketoacidosis at time of diagnosis of Type 1 diabetes in children and adolescents: effect of a national prevention campaign. Arch Pediatr. 2015;22(4):343–51.
4. Szypowska A, Ramotowska A, Grzechnik-Gryziak M, Szypowski W, Pasierb A, Piechowiak K. High frequency of diabetic ketoacidosis in children with newly diagnosed type 1 diabetes. J Diabetes Res. 2016;2016:9582793. https://doi.org/10.1155/2016/9582793.
5. Dabelea D, Rewers A, Stafford JM, Standiford DA, Lawrence JM, Saydah S, et al. Trends in the prevalence of ketoacidosis at diabetes diagnosis: the SEARCH for diabetes in youth study. Pediatrics. 2014;133(4):e938–45.
6. Deylami R, Townson J, Mann M, Gregory JW. Systematic review of publicity interventions to increase awareness amongst healthcare professionals and the public to promote earlier diagnosis of type 1 diabetes in children and young people. Pediatr Diabetes. 2018;19(3):566–73.
7. Jawaid A, Sohaila A, Mohammad N, Rabbani U. Frequency, clinical characteristics, biochemical findings and outcomes of DKA at the onset of type-1 DM in young children and adolescents living in a developing country – an experience from a pediatric emergency department. J Pediatr Endocrinol Metab. 2019;32(2):115–9.
8. Onyiriuka AN, Ifebi E. Ketoacidosis at diagnosis of type 1 diabetes in children and adolescents: frequency and clinical characteristics. J Diabetes Metab Disord. 2013;12:47. https://doi.org/10.1186/2251-6581-12-47.
9. Poovazhagi V. Risk factors for mortality in children with diabetic ketoacidosis from developing countries. World J Diabetes. 2014;5:932–8.
10. Jasper SU, Opara CM, Pyiki BE. Prevalence and clinical pattern of acute and chronic complications in African diabetic patients. Br J Med Med Res. 2014;4(30):4908–17.
11. Khunti K, Alsifri S, Aronson R, Cigrovski Berkovic M, Enters-Weijnen C, et al. on behalf of the HAT Investigator Group. Rates and predictors of hypoglycaemia in 27 585 people from 24 countries with insulin-treated type 1 and type 2 diabetes: the global HAT study. Diabetes. Obes Metab. 2016;18:907–15.
12. Jacqueminet S, Barthélémy O, Le Feuvre C. Screening of silent myocardial ischemia in Type 2 diabetic patients. A randomized trial comparing isotopic and echocardiographic stress tests. Diabetes Care. 2010;33(6):e79.

13. Guo W, Li M, Dong Y, Zhou H, Zhang Z, et al. Diabetes is a risk factor for the progression and prognosis of COVID-19. Diabetes Metab Res. 2020;4:395–403. https://doi.org/10.1002/dmrr.3319.
14. Fadini GP, Morieri ML, Longato E, et al. Prevalence and impact of diabetes among people infected with SARS-CoV-2. J Endocrinol Investig. 2020;43:867–9. https://doi.org/10.1007/s40618-020-01236-2.
15. World Health Organization. Cardiovascular Diseases (CVD). Key facts. https://www.who.int/en/news-room/fact-sheets/detail/cardiovascular-diseases-(cvds). Accessed 01 Apr 2020.
16. Gerstein HC. Diabetes: Dysglycaemia as a cause of cardiovascular outcomes. Nat Rev Endocrinol. 2015;11(9):508–10.
17. Emerging Risk Factors Collaboration, Sarwar N, Gao P, Seshasai SRK, Gobin R, Kaptoge S, et al. Diabetes mellitus, fasting blood glucose concentration, and risk of vascular disease: a collaborative meta-analysis of 102 prospective studies. Lancet. 2010;375(9733):2215–22.
18. Kondapally R, Seshasai S, Kaptoge S, Thompson A, Di Angelantonio E, Gao P, Sarwar N, et al. Diabetes mellitus, fasting glucose, and risk of cause-specific death. N Engl J Med. 2011;364(9):829–41.
19. Ballotari P, Ranieri SC, Luberto F, et al. Sex differences in cardiovascular mortality in diabetics and nondiabetic subjects: a population-based study (Italy). Int J Endocrinol. 2015;2015:914057. https://doi.org/10.1155/2015/914057.
20. Einarson TR, Acs A, Ludwig C, Panton UH. Prevalence of cardiovascular disease in type 2 diabetes: a systematic literature review of scientific evidence from across the world in 2007-2017. Cardiovasc Diabetol. 2018;17(1):83. https://doi.org/10.1186/s12933-018-0728-6.
21. Nair M, Prabhakaran D. Why do South Asians have high risk for CAD? Glob Heart. 2012;7:307–14.
22. Smokovski I, Milenkovic T, Trapp C, Mitov A. Diabetes care in the Republic of Macedonia: challenges and opportunities. Ann Global Health. 2015;81(6):792–802.
23. The Sixth Joint Task Force of the European Society of Cardiology and Other Societies on Cardiovascular Disease Prevention in Clinical Practice (constituted by representatives of 10 societies and by invited experts). 2016 European Guidelines on cardiovascular disease prevention in clinical practice. Eur Heart J. 2016;37:2315–2381.
24. Sabanayagam C, Banu R, Chee ML, Lee R, Wang YX, Tan G, et al. Incidence and progression of diabetic retinopathy: a systematic review. Lancet Diabetes Endocrinol. 2019;7(2):140–9.
25. Scanlon PH. The English national screening programme for sight-threatening diabetic retinopathy. J Med Screen. 2008;15(1):1–4.
26. Leese GP, Morris AD, Olson J. A national retinal screening programme for diabetes in Scotland. Diabet Med. 2003;20(12):962–4.
27. International Diabetes Federation. D-Net Diabetes Network for Healthcare Professionals. Artificial Intelligence and Screening for Diabetic Retinopathy. 2019. https://d-net.idf.org/en/discussions/182-artificial-intelligence-and-screening-for-diabetic-retinopathy.html.Accessed 11 April 2020.
28. World Health Organization. World report on vision. Geneva: World Health Organization; 2019.
29. Wu B, et al. Understanding CKD among patients with T2DM: prevalence, temporal trends, and treatment patterns-NHANES 2007-2012. BMJ Open Diabetes Res Care. 2016;4(1):e000154.
30. Alsahli M, Gerich JE. Hypoglycemia, chronic kidney disease, and diabetes mellitus. Mayo Clinic Proc. 2014;89:1564–71.
31. American Diabetes Association. Standards of medical care in diabetes, 2020. Diabetes Care. 2020;43(1):s1–212.
32. Li R, Bilik D, Brown MB, Zhang P, Ettner SL, Ackermann RT, et al. Medical costs associated with type 2 diabetes complications and comorbidities. Am J Manag Care. 2013;19(5):421–30.
33. Ali Z, Ahmed SM, Bhutto AR, Chaudhry A, Munir SM. Peripheral artery disease in type II diabetes. J Coll Physicians Surg Pak. 2012;22(11):686–9.
34. Akram J, Aamir A, Basit A, Qureshi MS, Mehmood T, Shahid SK, et al. Prevalence of peripheral arterial disease in type 2 diabetics in Pakistan. J Pak Med Assoc. 2011;61(7):644–8.

35. Yost M. Critical limb ischemia, Volume I. United States Epidemiology 2016 supplement. The Sage Group: Atlanta; 2016. http://thesagegroup.us/pages/reports/cli-us-supplement-2016.php. Accessed 16 March 2020

36. Hirsch AT, Criqui MH, Treat-Jacobson D, Regensteiner JG, Creager MA, Olin JW, et al. Peripheral arterial disease detection, awareness, and treatment in primary care. JAMA. 2001;286(11):1317–24.

37. Hasan R, Firwana B, Elraiyah T, Domecq JP, Prutsky G, Nabhan M, et al. A systematic review and meta-analysis of glycemic control for the prevention of diabetic foot syndrome. J Vas Surg. 2016;63(2 Supplement):22S–28S.e2.

38. Davies M, Brophy S, Williams R, Taylor A. The prevalence, severity, and impact of painful diabetic peripheral neuropathy in type 2 diabetes. Diabetes Care. 2006;29(7):1518–22.

39. Fowkes FG, Rudan D, Rudan I, et al. Comparison of global estimates of prevalence and risk factors for peripheral artery disease in 2000 and 2010: a systematic review and analysis. Lancet. 2013;382:1329–40.

40. Shah AD, Langenberg C, Rapsomaniki E, et al. Type 2 diabetes and incidence of cardiovascular diseases: a cohort study in 1.9 million people. Lancet Diabetes Endocrinol. 2015;3:105–13.

41. Hiramoto JS, Katz R, Weisman S, et al. Gender-specific risk factors for peripheral artery disease in a voluntary screening population. J Am Heart Assoc. 2014;3:e000651.

42. Thiruvoipati T, Kielhorn CE, Armstrong EJ. Peripheral artery disease in patients with diabetes: epidemiology, mechanisms, and outcomes. World J Diabetes. 2015;6:961–9.

43. Moxey PW, Gogalniceanu P, Hinchliffe RJ, Loftus IM, Jones KJ, Thompson MM, et al. Lower extremity amputations--a review of global variability in incidence. Diabet Med. 2011;28(10):1144–53.

44. Amoah VMK, Anokye R, Acheampong E, Dadson HR, Osei M, Nadutey A. The experiences of people with diabetes related lower limb amputation at the Komfo Anokye Teaching Hospital (KATH) in Ghana. BMC Res Notes. 2018;11(1):66. https://doi.org/10.1186/s13104-018-3176-1.

45. Mishra SC, Chhatbar KC, Kashikar A, Mehndiratta A. Diabetic foot. BMJ. 2017;359:j5064. https://doi.org/10.1136/bmj.j5064.

46. Zhang P, Lu J, Jing Y, Tang S, Zhu D, Bi Y. Global epidemiology of diabetic foot ulceration: a systematic review and meta-analysis. Ann Med. 2017;49(2):106–16.

47. Driver VR, Fabbi M, Lavery LA, Gibbons G. The costs of diabetic foot: the economic case for the limb salvage team. J Vasc Surg. 2010;52(3 Suppl):17S–22S.

48. Chapman D, Foxcroft R, Dale-Harris L, Ronte H, Bidgoli F, Bellary S. Insights for care: the healthcare utilisation and cost impact of managing Type 2 diabetes-associated microvascular complications. Diabetes Ther. 2019;10(2):575–85.

49. Cavan D, Makaroff L, da Rocha FJ, Sylvanowicz M, Ackland P, Conlon J, et al. The Diabetic Retinopathy Barometer Study: global perspectives on access to and experiences of diabetic retinopathy screening and treatment. Diabetes Res Clin Pract. 2017;129:16–24.

50. Express.co.uk: Diabetes warning: epidemic may 'bankrupt the NHS'. 2019. https://www.express.co.uk/life-style/health/1201749/Diabetes-warning-NHS-latest-migrants. Accessed 01 April 2020.

51. Smokovski I, Milenkovic T, Cho HN. First stratified diabetes prevalence data for Republic of Macedonia derived from the National eHealth System. Diabetes Res Clin Pract. 2018;143:179–83.

52. Williams R, Van Gaal L, Lucioni C. CODE-2 Advisory Board. Assessing the impact of complications on the costs of Type II diabetes. Diabetologia. 2002;45(7):S13–7.

53. American Diabetes Association. Economic Costs of Diabetes in the U.S. in 2017. Diabetes Care. 2018;41(5):917–28.

54. von Ferber L, Köster I, Hauner H. Medical costs of diabetic complications total costs and excess costs by age and type of treatment results of the German CoDiM Study. Exp Clin Endocrinol Diabetes Off J Ger Soc Endocrinol Ger Diabetes Assoc. 2007;115(2):97–104.

55. Kähm K, Laxy M, Schneider U, Rogowski WH, Lhachimi SK, Holle R. Health care costs associated with incident complications in patients with Type 2 diabetes in Germany. Diabetes Care. 2018;41(5):971–8.
56. Alva ML, Gray A, Mihaylova B, Leal J, Holman RR. The impact of diabetes-related complications on healthcare costs: new results from the UKPDS (UKPDS 84). Diabet Med J Br Diabet Assoc. 2015;32(4):459–66.
57. Marcellusi A, Viti R, Sciattella P, Aimaretti G, De Cosmo S, Provenzano V, et al. Economic aspects in the management of diabetes in Italy. BMJ Open Diabetes Res Care. 2016;4(1):e000197.
58. Zhuo X, Zhang P, Hoerger TJ. Lifetime direct medical costs of treating type 2 diabetes and diabetic complications. Am J Prev Med. 2013;45(3):253–61.
59. Riddle MC, Herman WH. The cost of diabetes care – an elephant in the room. Diabetes Care. 2018;41(5):929–32.
60. Seuring T, Archangelidi O, Suhrcke M. The economic costs of type 2 diabetes: a global systematic review. PharmacoEconomics. 2015;33:811–31.
61. Li R, Zhang P, Barker LE, Chowdhury FM, Zhang X. Cost-effectiveness of interventions to prevent and control diabetes mellitus: a systematic review. Diabetes Care. 2010;33(8):1872–94.
62. Bommer C, Heesemann E, Sagalova V, Manne-Goehler J, Atun R, Bärnighausen T, et al. The global economic burden of diabetes in adults aged 20-79 years: a cost-of-illness study. Lancet Diabetes Endocrinol. 2017;5(6):423–30.

Chapter 4
Cost-Effectiveness of Available Diabetes Treatments

Insulin treatment has been a life-saving and only medication for type 1 diabetes for almost a century. It was already explained that the burden of diabetes prevalence is largely due to the steep rise in the number of people with type 2 diabetes. For type 2 diabetes, most of the current guidelines recommend metformin as initial treatment. Metformin is a generic, relatively cheap and affordable diabetes medication. Since diabetes is a progressive condition, there is often a need to intensify the treatment after metformin.

According to the relevant guidelines, selection of medication to be added after metformin is based on several factors, including individual characteristics, presence of established atherosclerotic cardiovascular disease (ASCVD) or high ASCVD risk, other comorbidities, potential for weight gain, hypoglycemia, safety, tolerability, and the cost of medication [1].

Insulin remains the most effective diabetes medication and several improvements were made to the amino acid sequence of insulin molecule to enhance its properties, which resulted in the designer insulins or insulin analogues. Insulin analogues are characterized by faster onset and higher peak of action when administered subcutaneously compared to human insulin—bolus insulin analogues; or by prolonged duration of action, smoother and peakless profile—basal insulin analogues. First bolus insulin analogue was introduced in 1996, and first basal insulin analogue was introduced in 2000. Insulin analogues are usually offered at higher prices compared to human insulins and although they make the standard treatment for the majority of population with diabetes in developed countries, a lot of individuals in developing countries are still treated with human insulins.

The cost of insulin has been constantly rising in the past two decades [1, 2]. Unfortunately, in many countries insulin is not completely reimbursed and its high prices become a significant burden for the people with diabetes. This results in higher 'out-of pocket' expenditures, and contributes to a significant treatment non-adherence with devastating consequences [1, 2].

The cost of diabetes treatment, including insulin therapy, is a major factor in the cost-effective diabetes management. There is a huge discrepancy in the availability

© Springer Nature Switzerland AG 2021
I. Smokovski, *Managing Diabetes in Low Income Countries*,
https://doi.org/10.1007/978-3-030-51469-3_4

of diabetes treatments between developed and developing countries. And even more tragic is that this is also relevant for the insulin treatment.

According to the global survey conducted by the IDF in 2016, metformin and sulfonylureas, as the most widely prescribed classes of oral antidiabetic treatment, were always available in over 80% of high-income countries, compared with less than 20% in low-income countries [3]. The situation with insulin in low-income countries is even worse—insulin, in its various types, was always available when and where needed in over 80% of high-income countries, compared with less than 15% in low-income countries [3].

The IDF survey has been an eye-opener for various stakeholders that many people with diabetes in developing countries do not have uninterrupted access to basic antidiabetic medication, including insulin as a life-saving medication [3].

A lot of people with diabetes, even in the most developed country of the world—the US, are struggling with the affordability of insulin treatment. According to the latest reports, 1 in 4 people with diabetes in the US is rationing the insulin supplies [4]. The reason has been the rising cost of insulin, and such rationing could potentially result in tragic consequences [4].

The example of insulin affordability makes the distinction between developed and developing countries quite ambiguous. There are developing countries where insulins are completely reimbursed for all people with diabetes requiring insulin treatment, relevant for both human insulins and insulin analogues (e.g. the Republic of North Macedonia), and developed countries where considerable share of people with diabetes have to copay for insulin.

Initiatives are underway in several US states for limiting the insulin copayments per certain amount monthly. The legislation would create a program allowing states to procure insulin supplies at discounted prices and dispense them without prescription renewals in selected cases.

That was certainly not the intention of the bright minds that discovered the insulin back in 1921. Banting and Best vision was that everyone who needed insulin would be able to afford it, which is why they sold the insulin patent to the University of Toronto for just a dollar. Nearly 100 years later, many people with diabetes have to pay significant amounts for their insulin medication [4].

In the past two decades, prices for the most commonly prescribed insulins have increased by more than 700% in the US after adjusting for inflation [4]. It is not quite transparent, which are the factors that have contributed to such increase in the price of insulin treatment [4]. It has been reported in the US that people with diabetes with annual income below USD 100,000 were more likely to ration insulin compared to people with incomes above this level [4]. Such rationing was associated with inadequate glycaemic control [4].

Innovation has often been cited as a reason for the rising insulin costs; however, the price of the same insulins has increased several folds in the past 20 years. If a long-term affordability of life-saving medication cannot be guaranteed in the US, it would certainly be a challenge for a large part of the population with diabetes in developing countries.

It is not only the medication - the other diabetes related costs exert an additional financial burden. People with diabetes in the US are experiencing more financial issues than those without diabetes, even when they have healthcare insurance [4]. Nearly 40% of people with diabetes reported financial challenges from medical costs, including medical debt or the inability to afford needed medical care [4]. This challenge was associated with high financial distress, food insecurity, treatment non-adherence, and missed or delayed medical care [4].

The importance of affordability of diabetes medication, and insulin treatment in particular, is emphasized in times of global crisis as during the latest pandemic with COVID-19. There is a risk of production and supply shortages of this critical medication, making the people with diabetes concerned about the availability of insulin treatment. Another factor is the increasing unemployment rate, affecting the healthcare insurance and financial resources of the people with diabetes, and their access to the life-saving medication.

People with diabetes in developed countries might experience difficulties with the access to diabetes treatment, including insulin treatment. Understandably, the situation is worse in the lower resource countries. Most of the novel treatments that have demonstrated benefits in people with established CVD, such as GLP-1RA and SGLT2i, are largely unavailable in developing countries due to their cost.

A huge problem with the access to medications is that price is usually similar in both developed and developing countries. In other words, global pharmaceutical companies are not adjusting their prices for the economic strength of the country. On the contrary, many of them challenged by the reference pricing system where prices in one country are used as a reference for prices in other countries are persistent in not adjusting the prices according to the local circumstances. In doing so, they try to prevent a domino-effect on prices across major geographical areas and markets. If faced with the possibility of reduction of prices, pharmaceutical companies are battling to keep them unchanged in the countries where they operate.

To put it in another perspective, pharmaceutical companies do not offer lower prices for medicines adjusted for the wealth of the country, thus making certain therapeutic options unaffordable for the majority of population with diabetes in developing countries. Pharmaceutical companies justify such high prices with the huge costs of research and development and the calculated health economics benefit for the healthcare system if the medication is used, taking into consideration both direct and indirect costs.

The problem is that those prices and health economic benefits are often calculated based upon the input variables as financially valued in the most developed countries, which are the largest markets for the companies. The products are then offered at the similar prices in both developed and developing countries, although the financial value of input variables would be much lower in developing countries. Direct and indirect costs in developing countries are lower; however, the input for justifying the prices is based on the costs from the most developed countries.

That is the reason why, very often, health economics analysis of cost-effectiveness of diabetes treatment cannot justify the price offered for the developing countries.

In many instances prices are much higher than the perceived healthcare benefits of the medication in developing countries. Hence, it would be difficult to demonstrate cost-effectiveness of the novel diabetes treatments in the setting of developing countries. Taking into consideration that the overall market for most diabetes medications is usually shared by only few global pharmaceutical companies, the developing countries have no other choice but to procure the medication for the prices offered.

There are two possibilities for developing countries in that situation. The first possibility is to allow wider use and reimbursement of high priced diabetes treatments exerting huge pressure on the healthcare budget. The second possibility is to limit their use, leaving major parts of population with diabetes without effective treatment.

The first possibility when countries with limited resources are committed to provide novel diabetes therapeutic options, exerts not only enormous pressure on the healthcare budgets, but is leaving other healthcare areas facing potential shortages. Those areas include the other NCDs that are becoming more prevalent in developing countries. Diabetes related costs have huge impact even on the normal functioning of the hospitals. In such scenario, developing countries are forced to continuously borrow money to cover this gap in the healthcare budgets, making them severely indebted and vulnerable, but doing their best to keep the system afloat.

Even when choosing modern insulin treatment, such as the first or second generation basal insulin analogues, cost-effectiveness of the treatment has to be considered. We have to consider not only the cost of a pen or a pack, but also the units of insulin required to achieve comparable glycemic control. It has been demonstrated that for achieving comparable glycemic control with the two first generation basal analogues, required doses are quite different. That may result in a different cost of treatment per person [5].

In the light of the latest COVID-19 global pandemic when whole countries and economies have been in lockdown with rising unemployment; countries have to borrow money to keep the societies living, and additional borrowing for providing the most modern treatment would be a challenge for the healthcare systems.

The second possibility would mean lack of access to modern diabetes treatments which increases the risk of poor glycemic control and diabetes complications. Recent medications, such as SGLT2i and GLP-1RA, have demonstrated benefits beyond glycemic control and lack of those medications additionally increases the cardiovascular risk in people with type 2 diabetes.

The role of some pharmaceutical companies is not limited only to the pricing of diabetes medications in developing countries. Developing countries usually have less stringent regulatory requirements for sales and marketing, as well as for medical and clinical activities of the pharmaceutical companies. Consequently, physicians tend to adhere less to diabetes care guidelines in developing compared to developed countries.

The regulation is either insufficient or completely absent, and there are numerous examples of physicians from developing countries being incentivized by certain pharmaceutical companies to increase the prescriptions of medications. In most extreme cases, the diabetes care guidelines could be largely influenced by pharmaceutical companies' interests expressed through the scientific views of 'independent experts'.

It is worth mentioning the situation of global pharmaceutical companies running clinical trials in developing countries. In many cases, study fees received by physicians in developing countries are relatively high compared to their wages, and could be a potential source of scientific bias when performing clinical trials.

Unfortunately, some of the pharmaceutical companies are not separating their sales and marketing from their clinical activities, making the clinical trials not the necessity to generate reliable clinical data, but a powerful tool to have principal investigators on their side when pursuing sales and marketing objectives.

Not only the national healthcare decisions are affected where the principal investigators could potentially have a huge influence through advisory, guidelines, or national procurement procedures, but the science and medicine could be affected, since it is difficult to be reassured that generated clinical data would be of acceptable integrity.

One solution would be to conduct studies in developing countries by independent clinical research organizations, and to completely disconnect clinical from sales and marketing activities of the companies. In addition, there have to be strict regulation in the developing countries on the means of financing of physicians by pharmaceutical companies.

Some of the pharmaceutical companies exert their influence on the healthcare systems in developing countries through certain patient organizations which they are covertly funding. Instead of pharmaceutical companies appearing in public and fighting for the high priced novel diabetes treatments, it is often few people with diabetes attempting to win the public support by requiring novel treatment for this vulnerable population. It puts additional pressure on the policy makers and influences their decisions which rely less on the evidence based on the cost-effectiveness of the medication, and more on the huge noise generated in the public space.

Digital and social media have recently played an important role in facilitating these processes driven towards additional pressure on the healthcare budgets, especially in the developing countries. Information is spread very fast through the social media, and it leaves little or no room for any cost-effective analysis of the treatment in question under the particular health economics circumstances of the developing country.

Innovations are something no one can live without, that is for sure. Innovations in medicines are welcome; they have significantly contributed towards better medical outcomes and increased life expectancy. However, in order to provide sustainable diabetes care, cost-effectiveness of novel treatments has to be taken into consideration under the circumstances of the developing countries.

Very often, due to the practices mentioned above, the penetration of more expensive diabetes medication has been higher in developing compared to developed countries. One example was the situation in the Republic of North Macedonia. In 2011, insulin analogues were contributing with 84% of the total insulin volume and 92% of the total insulin value in the country, after continuous growth in the previous

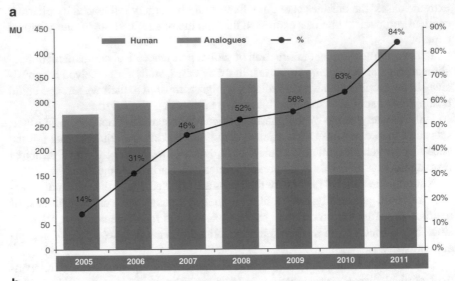

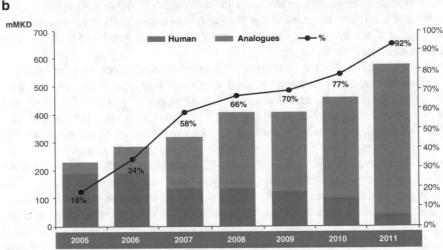

Fig. 4.1 Insulin volume (MU) and value (mMKD) in the Republic of North Macedonia, 2005–2011 [6]. (**a**) Insulin volume (MU), MU Mega Units. (**b**) Insulin value (mMKD), mMKD million Macedonian Denars

years (Fig. 4.1a, b) [6]. The penetration of the more expensive insulin analogues in the Republic of North Macedonia was higher compared to some of the most developed countries in the world, such as Germany or Norway (Fig. 4.2) [6].

The considerable increase in the penetration of insulin analogues, taking into consideration that insulins have been free of charge for the patients, was unbearable cost for the Healthcare Insurance Fund and Government Programs. Unfortunately, the high percentage of individuals using insulin analogues was not paralleled with the improvement of glycemic control or prevention of diabetes complications [7].

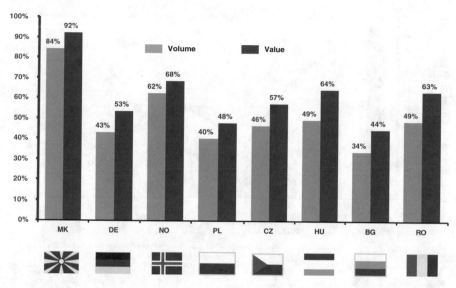

Fig. 4.2 Comparison of volume and value share of insulin analogues, 2011 [6]

On the contrary, people with diabetes were offered expensive insulin analogues free of charge with no or very limited possibility of glucose monitoring, since the test strips were quite expensive and were largely unavailable for the majority of people with diabetes. It was like driving the most expensive car in the world blindfolded. Such high penetration of insulin analogues was not mirrored by any monitoring of metabolic control parameters that are crucial for the prevention of diabetes complications.

To put the burden into broader context, if the cost for insulin analogues per person was analyzed in relation to the wealth of the country represented as GDP, and the index for Republic of North Macedonia was marked as 100, then the indices for the most developed countries in the world, such as Germany and Norway, would be 38 and 19 (Fig. 4.3a) [6]. Similar results were obtained if the cost of analogues was analyzed in relation to the GDP per person with diabetes (Fig. 4.3b) [6]. It means that the lower resource country, such as the Republic of North Macedonia, was paying three to five times more for modern diabetes treatment in relation to its wealth, in comparison with some of the most developed countries in Europe (Fig. 4.3) [6].

This situation is similar in other middle- or low-income countries, if we compare the healthcare resources allocated for modern treatment related to their wealth, to those of the developed countries.

It was already mentioned that 40% of all non-hospital medications reimbursed by the Healthcare Insurance Fund and Government Programs in Republic of North Macedonia, was spent on insulin and related supplies, such as insulin needles, glucagon, insulin pumps and ancillaries (Fig. 1.4). This cost did not include oral antidiabetic medication, other form of diabetes medication, or direct and indirect costs of diabetes complications. It is a great example of how the cost of diabetes medication could bankrupt a whole healthcare system of a developing country. The

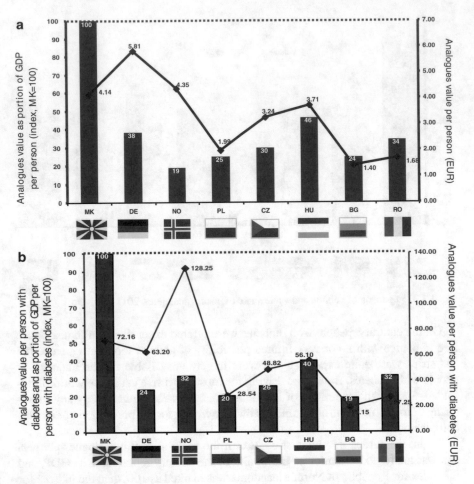

Fig. 4.3 Analogues value per person and as portion of GDP per person (index) (**a**), analogues value per person with diabetes and as portion of GDP per person with diabetes (index) (**b**), 2011 [6]

Fig. 4.4 Reduction of cost of insulin and related supplies in the Republic of North Macedonia, 2012–2016 [12]

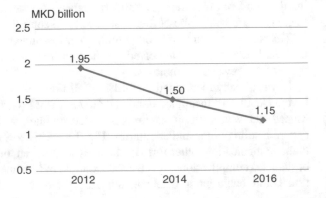

pressure is higher in reverse relation to the wealth of the country – lower resource countries are affected the most.

To put it into perspective, the cost of insulin and related supplies for 4 years was equal to the cost of the huge, modern clinical complex that was planned to be built in the capital of the Republic of North Macedonia, and to serve the needs of the entire population across all clinical disciplines [6].

The Republic of North Macedonia has been characterized by high insulin penetration, as 43.8% of all diagnosed people with diabetes were treated with insulin in 2015 (Table 1.1) [7]. The relatively high insulin penetration could be explained by the limited access to non-insulin treatments, such as DPP-4i, SGLT2i and GLP-1RA. Therefore, people with type 2 diabetes requiring treatment intensification after metformin and sulfonylureas were more rapidly initiated on insulin treatment.

The country introduced several initiatives, as already described, including a strategic National Diabetes Plan, adopting international diabetes care guidelines under the local circumstances and publishing those as National Diabetes Care guidelines in the Official Journal of the country, formation of National Diabetes Committee, responsible for monitoring of adherence to diabetes guidelines by various stakeholders, and integration of diabetes care modules in the NeHS [8–11].

According to the guidelines, people with type 2 diabetes requiring insulin treatment were required to start on human insulins first, and then, under certain circumstances, they were allowed to be transferred to more costly insulin analogues. No limitations on the use of insulin analogues in people with type 1 diabetes were stipulated with the national guidelines.

In addition, central procurement of insulin and related supplies was introduced, together with parallel imports. Insulin in all its forms was provided 100% free of charge. On the other hand, the number of free test strips was increased seven-fold for the people with diabetes on insulin treatment. National Diabetes Committee identified numerous cases of people with type 2 diabetes treated with insulin analogies and having poor glycemic control. In many of those, cheaper human insulins were found to be better alternative to insulin analogues in terms of glycemic control. Penetration of insulin analogue was reduced from over 90% to 55% in 4 years, resulting in considerable savings.

Public procurement at central level could also drive the prices down, instead of each hospital or region procuring diabetes treatment supplies on its own. Bigger quantities usually result in reduction of prices due to the increased volume. Ensuring there is a competition among bidders drives the prices down, although the competition might be limited for certain diabetes medications.

Biosimilars and generics increase competition resulting in reduction of prices, after the patents of originator diabetes treatments expire. Encouraging generics and biosimilars producing pharmaceutical companies to compete at the centrally organized procurements could contribute to the cost-savings.

The centralized, integrated NeHS had a crucial role in the monitoring of adherence to the National Diabetes Care guidelines. The significant increase in glucose monitoring resulted in reduction of acute diabetes emergencies.

Such rationalization of treatment costs allowed for inclusion of novel classes of diabetes treatment, such as DPP-4i, SGLT2i and GLP-1RA, that were provided free of charge for selected people with type 2 diabetes according to the Guidelines.

By implementing all above measures, the biannual cost of the national, centralized, public procurement of insulin, insulin needles, test strips, glucagon, insulin pumps and related ancillaries was reduced from MKD 1.95 billion in 2012 to MKD 1.5 billion in 2014, and MKD 1.15 billion in 2016, despite the increase in the number of people with diabetes, increase in the cumulative annual growth rate of insulin volume by 5% over the period, increase in the number of free test strips by sevenfold, and introduction of novel diabetes treatment classes, such as GLP-1RA, SGLT2i, and DPP-4i (Fig. 4.4) [12].

This rationalization of costs confirms that even in the developing countries there could be enough resources if those are spent rationally and by practicing the evidence based medicine. The released resources could be used for additional initiatives to fight diabetes, for increasing glucose monitoring capacity, or for introduction of novel classes of diabetes treatment.

Those cost reductions resulted in reduced profits for some of the pharmaceutical companies, fiercely attacking the diabetes care policies and the people behind them. Hence, everyone involved in any such initiative for cost rationalization has to be prepared to be fiercely attacked. Attacks are usually orchestrated through selected few people with diabetes, using mass and social media.

Insulin treatment has to be provided to every person in need. If evidence based medical guidelines are practiced by every physician, in addition to initiatives resulting in reduction of prices of diabetes medication, it is possible to provide sustainable diabetes care in a setting with limited resources.

> ***What should be done to provide cost-effective diabetes treatment in developing countries?***
> Each developing country should …
>
> - … secure adherence to the National Diabetes Care guidelines, including the prescription of diabetes treatment;
> - … consider central procurement of diabetes treatment while encouraging biosimilars, generics and parallel imports to reduce the prices;
> - … use centralized, integrated NeHS to evaluate the cost-effectiveness of treatment;
> - … allocate resources for sufficient glucose monitoring;
> - … consider introduction of novel diabetes treatment for selected people with diabetes, according to the Guidelines.

References

1. American Diabetes Association. Standards of medical care in diabetes 2020. Diabetes Care. 2020;43(1):s1–212.
2. Cefalu WT, Dawes DE, Gavlak G, et al. Insulin Access and Affordability Working Group. Conclusions and recommendations. Diabetes Care. 2018;41:1299–311.
3. International Diabetes Federation. Access to medicines and supplies for people with diabetes. Brussels: International Diabetes Federation; 2016.
4. International Diabetes Federation. Diabetes voice. Priced out: the impact of rising insulin costs, 03 Apr 2019. https://diabetesvoice.org/en/news/priced-out-the-impact-of-rising-insulin-costs/. Accessed 14 Mar 2020.
5. Rosenstock J, Davies M, Home DP, Larsen J, Koenen C, Schernthaner G. A randomised, 52-week, treat-to-target trial comparing insulin detemir with insulin glargine when administered as add-on to glucose-lowering drugs in insulin-naive people with type 2 diabetes. Diabetologia. 2008;51(3):408–16.
6. Smokovski I. National e-Health System – platform for preventive, predictive and personalized diabetes care, EPMA World Congress, Bonn, 03–05 September, 2015.
7. Smokovski I, Milenkovic T, Trapp C, Mitov A. Diabetes care in the Republic of Macedonia: challenges and opportunities. Ann Global Health. 2015;81(6):792–802.
8. Ministry of Health. Law on the Healthcare. Off J Repub Macedonia. 2015;10:12–88.
9. Ministry of Health. Guideline on healthcare related to the treatment and control of type 2 diabetes. Off J Repub Macedonia. 2015;40:15–34.
10. Health Consumer Powerhouse. Euro health consumer index report, 2014. Taby: Health Consumer Powerhouse. 2015. https://healthpowerhouse.com/media/EHCI-2014/EHCI-2014-report.pdf. Accessed 20 March 2020.
11. Velinov G, Jakimovski B, Lesovski D, Ivanova Panova D, Frtunik D, Kon-Popovska M. EHR system MojTermin: implementation and initial data analysis. Stud Health Technol Inform. 2015;210:872–6.
12. Smokovski I. The power of e-Health integration solutions. European Center for Peace and Development (ECPD). University for Peace by the United Nations. XXII ECPD International Summer School Management of Healthcare Institutions. Professional Management – the Key to Sustainability of European Healthcare, Bečići, Montenegro, 26–30 June 2017.

Chapter 5
Cost-Effectiveness of Monitoring Metabolic Control

What cannot be measured cannot be managed and improved—the golden rule of management is particularly true when it comes to managing diabetes. When we talk about measuring in diabetes, we primarily think of glucose monitoring.

In general, there have been three eras of glucose monitoring: from urine samples since the 1940s, from blood samples since the 1960s, and from interstitial fluid with sensors, i.e. continuous glucose monitoring (CGM) since the late 1990s. First compact blood glucose meter (BGM) with digital display and possibility of Self-Monitoring of Blood Glucose (SMBG) was introduced in the 1980s. Latest hybrid closed loop systems are integrating insulin delivery in a form of subcutaneous insulin infusion with the CGMs, and are adjusting the delivery of basal insulin automatically.

A 3-year study has recently reported that people with type 1 diabetes on insulin pumps and SMBG demonstrated worse glycaemic control compared to those on insulin pen therapy and CGM [1]. It suggested that metabolic control depends more on the frequency of glucose monitoring, and less on the method of delivering insulin [1]. Study results confirm that measuring glycaemia is a very critical part in the management of diabetes.

There has been a considerable increase in the CGM use by people with type 1 diabetes as reported from the real-world study T1D Exchange Registry from the US [2]. Percentage of people with type 1 diabetes on CGM from this Registry increased from 6% in 2011 to 31% in 2017 [2]. It is expected that by 2023, 87% of people with type 1 diabetes and 27% of people with type 2 diabetes on insulin treatment will be using CGMs in the US [2].

Taking into consideration the uptake of CGMs worldwide, the question is if SMBG is already dead. It is like asking a question if fossil fuel cars are already dead. According to the figures from 2018, only one in 250 cars on the roads was electric (0.4%), and the same percentage of people with diabetes were using CGM (0.4%) (Fig. 5.1) [3–5]. Despite the number of CGM users is growing considerably, mainly due to the increase in users of intermittently scanned CGM (isCGM), SMBG will not be dead in the foreseeable future. This is of particular importance for the

© Springer Nature Switzerland AG 2021
I. Smokovski, *Managing Diabetes in Low Income Countries*,
https://doi.org/10.1007/978-3-030-51469-3_5

	users globally 2018
Dexcom	> 450.000
Abbott	> 1.300.000
Senseonics	> 4.000
Medtronic	> 180.000
Total	> 1.934.000

Image by Gerd Altmann from Pixabay

… only one in 250 cars on the road is **electric (0.4%)**   … only one in 225 people with diabetes on **CGM (0.4%)**

Fig. 5.1 Estimated proportion of electric cars on road and people with diabetes using CGM, data adapted from Ref. [3–5]. CGM Continuous Glucose Monitoring

Table 5.1 Recommended glycaemic targets by ADA and IDF, data adapted from Ref. [8, 9]

	ADA	IDF
Preprandial capillary plasma glucose	4.4–7.2 mmol/L (80–130 mg/dL)	<6.0 mmol/L (108 mg/dL)
Peak postprandial capillary plasma glucose	<10.0 mmol/L (180 mg/dL)	<10.0 mmol/L (180 mg/dL)
	Correlate with HbA1c < 7.0% (53 mmol/mol)	

developing countries where the access to CGM is limited, or CGMs are not available at all, due to the much higher cost compared to SMBG.

Benefits of intensive glycaemic control on the reduction of diabetes complications in people with type 1 diabetes were initially demonstrated in the DCCT study, where SMBG was part of the multifactorial intervention [6]. Reduction in microvascular and macrovascular diabetes complications in the subjects from intensive group was also observed in the follow-up observational study EDIC (Epidemiology of Diabetes Interventions and Complications) [6].

Similar findings were reported for people with type 2 diabetes from the UKPDS and the follow-up UKPDS-PTM study, where the improvement of glycaemic control was associated with reduced risk for diabetes complications [7].

Frequent SMBG is key to achieve glycaemic targets as set by the international authorities, ADA and IDF (Table 5.1) [8, 9]. Achieving the recommended targets correlates with HbA1c below 7%, which is associated with reduced risk for diabetes complications.

Increased frequency of SMBG results in reduction of HbA1c in people with type 1 diabetes [10]. If SMBG is measured more frequently throughout the day, the glycaemic control is improved, which was demonstrated for all age groups [10].

Titration to target FPG by the use of SMBG also reduces HbA1c in insulin-treated people with type 2 diabetes [11–14]. Use of SMBG was critical for establishing the so-called 'Treat-to-Target' concept, whereby achieving the target FPG through titration of basal insulin results in HbA1c reduction associated with lower risk of diabetes complications.

Things become more complex when SMBG is used in non-insulin treated people with type 2 diabetes, as there are studies confirming that use of SMBG significantly improves glycaemic control or reduces hypoglycemia risk in these people, and studies that have not demonstrated such benefits with SMBG [15–28].

Cochrane conclusions from 2012 were that the overall effect of SMBG on glycaemic control in non-insulin treated people with type 2 diabetes is incremental up to six months after initiation, and subsides after 12 months of use [29].

Intuitively, it should be better to take a proactive approach and do SMBG in order to manage the glycaemic control. The opposite is to wait for months until the next visit at physician's office to have HbA1c measured (reactive approach), realize it was high and glycaemic control was inadequate, and there is nothing to be done since the value of HbA1c reflects the time period that has elapsed [30].

The recommendations on SMBG in non-insulin treated people with type 2 diabetes are described in the IDF Guidelines on Self-Monitoring of Blood Glucose in Non-Insulin-Treated Type 2 Diabetes [31]. The Guidelines introduced the concept of 'structured SMBG', or making sense of the SMBG in the management of diabetes.

In the Guidelines, it is recommended that SMBG should only be used if individuals with diabetes and their healthcare providers have the knowledge, skills and willingness to incorporate it into their diabetes care plan [31]. It should be considered at the time of diagnosis as part of individuals' education, and to facilitate timely treatment initiation and titration optimization [31].

Self-monitoring of blood glucose should also be considered as part of an ongoing diabetes self-management education [31]. Protocols for SMBG in terms of frequency per day and days per week need to be individualized to address specific requirements [31].

Targets to be achieved with SMBG should be agreed between the person with diabetes and the healthcare provider [31]. Use of SMBG requires an easy procedure for regular monitoring of performance and accuracy of BGM [31].

Structured SMBG in non-insulin treated people with type 2 diabetes is a critical component of diabetes education and treatment. It is vital for glycaemic assessment, behavioral change, optimization of therapy, and diabetes education and understanding, both for the healthcare provider and the person with diabetes [31]. In addition, structured SMBG has an impact on the metabolic control, safety, quality of life (QoL), and the economic burden [31].

The role of structured SMBG in non-insulin treated people with type 2 diabetes has been confirmed by the recently published 'The SMBG Study' where the structured SMBG provided improvements in glycaemic control of non-insulin treated people with type 2 diabetes [32]. This study has proved the value of SMBG in people with type 2 diabetes not on insulin, if structured SMBG is implemented.

All the studies mentioned above were using SMBG as a tool to achieve lower HbA1c, and by lowering HbA1c to reduce the risk of diabetes complications. The value of HbA1c is currently acknowledged as the gold standard for measuring the glycaemic control. Nevertheless, the question is how reliable is HbA1c as a surrogate marker, and what are its advantages and limitations?

Advantages of the use of HbA1c as a measure of glycaemic control include that it is easy to measure, relatively cheap, predictive of vascular complications, and helps management decisions [33]. Limitations of HbA1c include the facts it only provides an approximate measure of glycaemia, is unable to address glycaemic variability (GV) or hypoglycemia, 50% of the HbA1c value reflects the mean BG in the previous month, and is unreliable in certain conditions [33].

Those conditions are quite numerous, including: (1) comorbidities, such as anemia, accelerated red blood cells turnover, thalassemia, reticulocytosis, haemolysis, HIV infection, uraemia, hyperbilirubinemia, dyslipidemia, cirrhosis, hypothyroidism; (2) physiologic states, such as ageing and pregnancy; (3) medications or treatments, such as alcohol, opioids, vitamin C and E, aspirin, erythropoietin, dapsone, ribavirin, blood transfusions, hemodialysis, and (4) other circumstances, such as, different glycation rate, protein turnover, race and ethnicity, laboratory assay, glycaemic variability, smoking, mechanic heart valves, and use of exogenous testosterone [6, 33, 34].

In a real world clinical practice it is estimated that 14–25% of HbA1c results are misleading [6, 33, 34]. That is the reason we are moving beyond HbA1c as a standard of adequate metabolic control, and novel glucometrics are introduced with the wider use of CGMs. Those novel glucometrics include Time In Range (TIR, defined as time spent in range 3.9–10 mmol/L (70–180 mg/dL)), Time Below Range (TBR, defined as time spent below 3.9 mmol/L (70 mg/dL)), and Time Above Range (TAR, defined as time above 10 mmol/l (180 mg/dL)). For people with type 1 and type 2 diabetes, TIR should be more than 70%, TBR below 4% (time below 3.0 mmol/L (54 mg/dL) should be below 1%), and TAR below 25% (time above 13.3 mmol/L (250 mg/dL) should be below 5%) [34].

Other glucometrics include the time CGM was active, average glucose, Glucose Management Indicator (GMI)—formerly known as estimated HbA1c, GV, and Ambulatory Glucose Profile (AGP) [34].

It has been demonstrated by the use of DCCT data that TIR was associated with reduction of microvascular complications in people with type 1 diabetes [35]. Each 10% reduction in TIR was associated with increase in the risk of retinopathy by 64%, and microalbuminuria by 40% [35].

Similar findings were reported for the association between TIR and microvascular complications in people with type 2 diabetes—the higher the value of TIR, the lower the risk for retinopathy [36]. It was recently published that TIR was inversely associated with Carotid Intima Media Thickness in people with type 2 diabetes, suggesting it could be related not only with reduction of microvascular, but also of macrovascular complications [37].

These novel glucometrics could also be used with BGMs, which is of great importance for the developing countries where CGMs would not be widely available soon. Glucometrics, such as average glycaemia, glucose variability, standard day, ambulatory glucose profile, change in glucose over time, glucose distribution, and integration with other relevant data including medications, insulin doses, diet, physical activity, illness, stress, or travel, could all be retrieved from SMBG data of BGMs [30].

Use of the Smart Glucometers, which are sending the SMBG data into the cloud to be further analyzed, reported, and shared with family and healthcare providers, could be of great significance for the developing countries, where the uptake of CGMs is expected to be slower due to the associated cost. There are diabetes management systems that enable BGMs to send the SMBG data into the cloud for analyses and reports in the form of novel glucometrics.

Accuracy of BGMs is crucial as critical decisions are based on the SMBG values. Current standards for SMBG accuracy include those of Food and Drug Administration (FDA) and International Organization for Standardization (ISO) 15197–2013 [8]. Recent study comparing second generation basal insulin analogues in people with type 2 diabetes reported inaccuracy of the BGMs used during the very sensitive period of insulin titration [38, 39]. It was concluded that if such inaccuracies of BGMs occur in highly controlled clinical trial settings, we can imagine what happens in everyday life of people with diabetes, and how it might affect treatment decisions and overall glycaemic control.

There are many factors affecting the accuracy of SMBG that have to be considered, especially in developing countries. Those include: (1) higher and lower oxygen tension conditions (glucose oxidase monitors are sensitive to oxygen); (2) temperature (reaction is sensitive to temperature, all monitors have an acceptable temperature range); (3) interfering substances (uric acid, galactose, xylose, acetaminophen, L-dopa, vitamin C); (4) manufacturing defects (could lead to bias in hypoglycaemic, target, and hyperglycaemic range); (5) test strip lot-to-lot variation (lot-to-lot variations as high as 11% could occur while using the same BGM); (6) alternate site testing (particularly when glucose levels are changing rapidly); (7) skin contaminants (food sources, such as fruits, juices, sodas, milk; hand lotions); (8) counterfeit test strips (pre-owned or second-hand test strips should not be used) [8, 30].

In comparison of 17 models of BGMs that were available on the market, 9 had a Mean Absolute Relative Difference (MARD) above 10%, which is unacceptable accuracy [40]. Similar results were obtained when ISO 15197 standards were applied, when out of 18 BGM on the market, only 6 met the ISO standards on accuracy [8]. Although there was a huge difference between the accuracy of CGMs and SMBG at the beginning, latest models of CGMs have a MARD comparable to SMBG in the range of 8.1% to 10.6% [41].

Affordability of BGMs and test strips for monitoring blood glucose is particularly important in a time of global crisis, such as the recent one with COVID-19 pandemic. Disruption of the global economy could lead to delays in manufacturing and supply shortages, leaving the people with diabetes without their essential tools for managing hyperglycemia. On the other hand, inadequately managed hyperglycemia makes them more prone to developing severe forms of the infectious

COVID-19 disease and increases the risk for worse outcomes after contracting the infection.

In a study conducted in developing countries, glycaemic control in individuals with type 2 diabetes remained suboptimal, indicating a need for system changes and better organization of care to improve self-management and attainment of treatment goals [42]. This also refers to improvements in monitoring of glycaemia [42].

The importance of SMBG could be elucidated from the real-world evidence reported from the Republic of North Macedonia. Although, majority of the people with diabetes in the country were on insulin analogues by 2011, it was not associated with adequate glycaemic control at a national level. People with diabetes had very limited access to free, reimbursed test strips as only 50 free test strips per year were provided for those on insulin treatment.

In addition to the rationalization of insulin treatment, since 2015 the number of free test strips was increased seven-fold to 350 free test strips per year for people with type 2 diabetes on insulin treatment, whereas the people with type 1 diabetes were provided with 125 free test strips per month.

Test strips were procured through centralized procedure that resulted in a significant reduction of the price per test strip, as higher volumes were associated with lower prices. Bidders were obliged to provide BGMs, lancets and lancet devices free of charge. Procurement of the test strips was part of the general procurement procedure, including insulins, glucagon, insulin pumps, ancillaries, and novel classes of diabetes medications (SGLT2i, GLP-1RA, DPP-4i). The cost savings achieved for test strips were significant and comparable to the cost savings achieved with the diabetes medications.

The considerable increase in the number of free test strips was associated with reduction of acute diabetes emergencies, such as DKA and HHS. In only a year, the number of acute diabetic complications was reduced by 9%, despite the increase in the number of people with diabetes and those who were on insulin treatment (Fig. 5.2) [43].

Fig. 5.2 Reduction of acute diabetes emergencies, DKA and HHS, after seven-fold increase in free test strips for people with type 2 diabetes on insulin treatment [43]. DKA Diabetes ketoacidosis, HHS Hyperglycaemic Hyperosmolar State

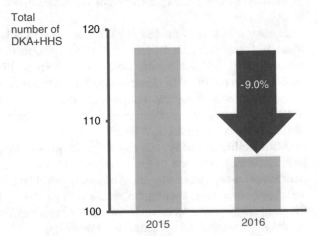

It confirms that is possible even in a setting with limited resources to increase the frequency of SMBG by considerably increasing the number of free test strips. Those actions could result in reduction of acute complications, and could potentially lower the risk for long-term diabetes complications through improved glycaemic control.

Above findings confirm the results from the COMISSAIR study that frequent measuring of glycaemia is critical for adequate glycaemic control, and more important than the method of insulin delivery [1]. If resources in diabetes care are limited, they should be adequately allocated for glucose monitoring. Each person has to be provided with a certain number of free or affordable test strips per month. It is equally important as the provision of free insulin.

Instead of fragmented procurement that is associated with lower volumes and higher prices, centralized procurement results in higher volumes and lower prices. Bidders who comply with the procurement specification could be included in the negative bidding process where they are competing by lowering the price, preferably using an electronic bidding system.

Reduced diabetes comorbidities by the frequent use of SMBG was reported from India, demonstrated to have economic and QoL implications [44]. In a simulation analysis, the cohort with at least one SMBG per day was associated with a 10-year estimated saving of INR 120,173 compared to the cohort with no SMBG [44].

Proactive diabetes management with SMBG was demonstrated to improve treatment outcomes and reduce morbidity and mortality in this simulation from India [44]. Near-normal BG levels could bring in cost savings from reduced long-term complications and avoidance of repeated hospitalizations along with an improved QoL [44].

Low adherence to the use of SMBG was reported even in people with type 1 diabetes from developed countries, such as Sweden [45]. In a survey study done before the wider use of CGMs in Sweden, it was reported that less than 50% of people with type 1 diabetes perform SMBG at least 4 times per day, according to the ADA guidelines, and 30% of people were unaware of the guidelines at all. The top two most reported reasons for not performing more frequent SMBG were 'not remembering' and 'lack of time' [45].

There is an underutilization of SMBG in people with type 2 diabetes from developed countries. Recent real-world study on the use of SMBG in people with type 2 diabetes from Italy concluded that there is an urgent need for improvement [46]. Non-insulin treated people with type 2 diabetes were using 15–23 test strips per month, people treated with basal insulin were using 32 test strips per month, and people with type 2 diabetes on basal-bolus insulin treatment were using 53–58 test-strips per month [46]. Similar findings were reported from other developed countries, such as Canada, the UK and France [47–49].

Unfortunately, there is a low rate of SMBG adherence according to the national guidelines, in both developed and developing countries. According to the available survey based studies, the rate of adherence was reported to be 28% in China, 39% in South and Central America, 50% in the UK, 52% in the US, and 59% in Jordan [50–52].

The rate of adherence was reported to be 58% in the recent study of real-world use of SMBG in people with type 2 diabetes in China [53]. It was not a survey based study and the SMBG was automatically recorded in a real-time manner by using a blood glucose monitoring platform [53]. For the first time intelligent BGMs were used to record the SMBG in people with type 2 in a real-time manner; unlike the survey based studies before that were relying on individuals' memory of the SMBG frequency [53].

Inadequate utilization of SMBG in people with type 2 diabetes mellitus in Sub-Saharan Africa has also been reported [54]. Based on 15 real-world, observational studies, it was found that percentage of people with type 2 diabetes able to do SMBG at home, ranges from 0% in Uganda, 3% to 10% in Ethiopia, 4% in Zimbabwe, 5% in Ghana, 20% in Kenya, 25% in Sudan, 26% in Tanzania, and 32% to 43% in Nigeria [54].

On average, only 15% of all people with type 2 diabetes in Sub-Saharan Africa were doing SMBG at home. Most of those people possessing BGMs at home performed SMBG only once a month, or at no regular interval, not adhering to the guidelines. In addition, only 1% to 2% of those people measured their blood glucose on a daily basis [54].

Only half of the people who performed SMBG at home, also kept records of their results, so they could analyze and discuss them with the healthcare providers as part of the structured SMBG process. There has been no study on the use of structured SMBG, i.e. of individuals' ability to analyze SMBG results and whether they know what to do if their blood glucose is above or below agreed target values [54].

In many developing countries test strips for SMBG are only available in private clinics where people with diabetes are financially capable to afford SMBG, and not in public clinics where test strips are not covered by public healthcare insurance. Understandably, glycaemic control is much better in private clinics compared to clinics with limited or no access to SMBG. In many developing countries, CGMs are not available at all [55].

In a small number of developing countries CGMs are available, but only to those on the most expensive healthcare insurance who can afford the consumables. As a result, almost everyone is on SMBG—and even then, getting enough test strips in public healthcare is very difficult [55].

Additionally to monitoring glycaemic control via HbA1c and novel glucometrics, it is vital to monitor other parameters important for adequate metabolic control, such as the lipid profile, SBP and DBP, BMI, smoking status, creatinine and UACR, and the other related laboratory parameters. Such information needs to be recorded in the individual EHRs of a centralized, integrated e-Health system.

Integration of BGM or CGM data into the individual EHRs could further facilitate the monitoring of glucose control in people with diabetes. Despite the novel technologies for measuring glycaemia, the vast majority of people with diabetes are using SMBG: The frequent use of SMBG and the novel glucometrics in the countries with limited resources could significantly contribute to the improved glycaemic control and reduced risk for diabetes complications.

> **What should be done to provide cost-effectiveness of monitoring of metabolic control in developing countries?**
> Each developing country should…
>
> - …ensure adequate number of free or affordable test strips for people with diabetes, primarily those who are on insulin treatment;
> - …consider central procurement of test strips to achieve reduction of prices;
> - …introduce the concept of structured SMBG for improved glycaemic control;
> - …ensure that healthcare providers and people with diabetes are familiar with the measures of SMBG accuracy;
> - …ensure that healthcare providers and people with diabetes are familiar with the novel glucometrics,
> - …ensure the metabolic control parameters are recorded in the individual EHRs, and continuously monitored.

References

1. Šoupal J, Petruželková L, Grunberger G, Hásková A, Flekač M, et al. Glycemic outcomes in adults with T1D are impacted more by continuous glucose monitoring than by insulin delivery method: 3 years of follow-up from the COMISAIR study. Diabetes Care. 2020;43(1):37–43.
2. Beck WR. Pains and gains in continuous glucose monitoring. Continuous glucose monitoring is trending – device options and utilizations. ADA 79th Scientific Sessions, 09 Jun 2019, San Francisco, United States. https://professional.diabetes.org/webcast/continuous-glucose-monitoring-trending%E2%80%94device-options-and-utilization. Accessed 17 Mar 2020.
3. International Diabetes Federation. IDF Diabetes Atlas. 9th ed. Brussels, Belgium: International Diabetes Federation; 2019.
4. Coren JM. Researchers have no idea when electric cars are going to take over, 2019. https://qz.com/1620614/electric-car-forecasts-are-all-over-the-map. Accessed 07 Oct 2019.
5. Garg S. Real time continuous glucose monitoring. New clinical outcomes, progress toward automated insulin delivery and trendsetting with interoperability. ADA 79th Scientific Sessions, 08 Jun 2019, San Francisco, United States. https://cgmeducation.net/Speaker_Ready.php. Accessed 01 Apr 2019.
6. Nathan MD for the DCCT/EDIC Research Group. The diabetes control and complications trial/epidemiology of diabetes interventions and complications study at 30 years: overview. Diabetes Care. 2014;37(1):9–16.
7. Holman RR, Paul SK, Bethel MA, Matthews DR, Neil HA. 10-year follow-up of intensive glucose control in type 2 diabetes. N Engl J Med. 2008;359(15):1577–89.
8. American Diabetes Association. Standards of medical care in diabetes 2020. Diabetes Care. 2020;43(1):s1–212.
9. IDF Clinical Practice Recommendations for managing Type 2 Diabetes in Primary Care, 2017. www.idf.org/managing-type2-diabetes. Accessed 10 Mar 2020.
10. Miller KM, Beck RW, Bergenstal RM, et al. Evidence of a strong association between frequency of self-monitoring of blood glucose and hemoglobin A1c levels in T1D exchange clinic registry participants. Diabetes Care. 2013;36:2009–14.
11. Riddle M, et al. The treat-to-target trial: randomized addition of glargine or human NPH insulin to oral therapy of type 2 diabetic patients. Diabetes Care. 2003;26:3080–6.
12. Yki-Järvinen H, et al. Insulin glargine or NPH combined with metformin in type 2 diabetes: the LANMET study. Diabetologia. 2006;49:442–51.

13. Bretzel RG, et al. Once-daily basal insulin glargine versus thrice-daily prandial insulin lispro in people with type 2 diabetes on oral hypoglycemic agents (APOLLO): an open randomised controlled trial. Lancet. 2008;371:1073–84.

14. Janka H, et al. Comparison of basal insulin added to oral agents versus twice-daily premixed insulin as initial insulin therapy for type 2 diabetes. Diabetes Care. 2005;28:254–9.

15. Martin S, et al. Self-monitoring of blood glucose in type 2 diabetes and long-term outcome: an epidemiological cohort study. Diabetologia. 2006;49:271–8.

16. Karter AJ, et al. Longitudinal study of new and prevalent use of self-monitoring of blood glucose. Diabetes Care. 2006;29:1757–63.

17. Bosi E, et al. Intensive structured self-monitoring of blood glucose and glycemic control in non-insulin treated type 2 diabetes: the PRISMA randomized trial. Diabetes Care. 2013;36(10):2887–94.

18. Schwedes U, et al. Meal-related structured self-monitoring of blood glucose: effect on diabetes control in non-insulin-treated type 2 diabetic patients. Diabetes Care. 2002;25:1928–32.

19. Barnett AH, et al. The efficacy of self-monitoring of blood glucose in the management of patients with type 2 diabetes treated with a gliclazide modified release-based regimen. A multicentre, randomized, parallel-group, 6-month evaluation (DINAMIC 1 study). Diabetes Obes Metab. 2008;10(12):1239–47.

20. Guerci B, et al. Self-monitoring of blood glucose significantly improves metabolic control in patients with type 2 diabetes mellitus: the Auto-Surveillance Intervention Active (ASIA) study. Diabetes Metab. 2003;29(6):587–94.

22. Polonsky WH, et al. Structured self-monitoring of blood glucose significantly reduces A1C levels in poorly controlled, non-insulin treated type 2 diabetes: results from the Structured Testing Program study. Diabetes Care. 2011;34:262–7.

22. Franciosi M, et al. ROSES: role of self-monitoring of blood glucose and intensive education in patients with Type 2 diabetes not receiving insulin. A pilot randomized clinical trial. Diabet Med. 2011;28:789–96.

23. Durán A, et al. Benefits of self-monitoring blood glucose in the management of new-onset Type 2 diabetes mellitus: the St Carlos Study, a prospective randomized clinic-based interventional study with parallel groups. J Diabetes. 2010;2:203–11.

24. Davis WA, et al. Does self-monitoring of blood glucose improve outcome in type 2 diabetes? The Fremantle Diabetes Study. Diabetologia. 2007;50:510–5.

25. Franciosi M, et al. The impact of blood glucose self-monitoring on metabolic control and quality of life in type 2 diabetic patients: an urgent need for better educational strategies. Diabetes Care. 2001;24:1870–7.

26. Davidson MB, et al. The effect of self-monitoring of blood glucose concentrations on glycated hemoglobin levels in diabetic patients not taking insulin: a blinded, randomized trial. Am J Med. 2005;118:422–5.

27. O'Kane MJ, et al. Efficacy of self-monitoring of blood glucose in patients with newly diagnosed type 2 diabetes (ESMON study): randomised controlled trial. BMJ. 2008;336:1174–7.

28. Farmer A, et al. Impact of self-monitoring of blood glucose in the management of patients with non-insulin treated diabetes: open parallel group randomised trial. BMJ. 2007;335:132. https://doi.org/10.1136/bmj.39247.447431.BE.

29. Malanda UL, et al. Self-monitoring of blood glucose in patients with type 2 diabetes mellitus who are not using insulin. Cochrane Database Syst Rev. 2012;18:CD005060.

30. AACE/ACE. Outpatient glucose monitoring consensus statement. Endocr Pract. 2016;22(2):231–61.

31. International Diabetes Federation. Self-monitoring of blood glucose in non-insulin-treated type 2 diabetes guidelines. International Diabetes Federation, 2009.

32. Parsons, et al. Effect of structured self-monitoring of blood glucose, with and without additional TeleCare support, on overall glycaemic control in non-insulin treated Type 2 diabetes: the SMBG Study, a 12-month randomized controlled trial. Diabet Med. 2019;36:578–90.

33. Ajjan RA. How can we realize the clinical benefits of continuous glucose monitoring? Diabetes Technol Therap. 2017;19(2):s27–36.

34. Battelino T, et al. International consensus report. Clinical targets for continuous glucose monitoring data interpretation: recommendations from the international consensus on time in range. Diabetes Care. 2019;42:1593–603.

35. Beck RW, Bergenstal RM, Riddlesworth TD, et al. Validation of time in range as an outcome measure for diabetes clinical trials. Diabetes Care. 2019;42:400–6.

36. Lu J, et al. Association of time in range, as assessed by continuous glucose monitoring, with diabetic retinopathy in type 2 diabetes. Diabetes Care. 2018;41:2370–6.

37. Lu J, Ma X, Shen Y, Wu Q, Wang R, et al. Time in range is associated with carotid intima-media thickness in type 2 diabetes. Diabetes Technol Ther. 2020;22(2):72–8.

38. Philis-Tsimikas A, Klonoff CD, Khunti K, Bajaj SH, Leiter AL, et al. on behalf of the CONCLUDE Study Group. Risk of hypoglycaemia with insulin degludec versus insulin glargine U300 in insulin-treated patients with type 2 diabetes: the randomised, head-to-head CONCLUDE trial. Diabetologia. 2020; https://doi.org/10.1007/s00125-019-05080-9.

39. Del Prato S. How conclusive is the CONCLUDE trial? Diabetologia. 2020; https://doi.org/10.1007/s00125-020-05086-8.

40. Ekhlaspour L, et al. Comparative accuracy of 17 point-of-care glucose meters. J Diabetes Sci Technol. 2017;11(3):558–66.

41. Facchinetti A, et al. Continuous glucose monitoring sensors: past, present and future algorithmic challenges. Sensors. 2016; 16(12). pii: E2093.

42. Chan CHJ, Gagliardino JJ, Baik HS, Chantelot JM, Ferreira RGS, et al. on behalf of IDPMS Investigators. Multifaceted Determinants for Achieving Glycemic Control The International Diabetes Management Practice Study (IDMPS). Diabetes Care. 2009;32:227–33.

43. Smokovski I. Self-monitoring as an important tool in preventing diabetes complications – evidence from the real world. International Diabetes Federation Congress, 02–06 Dec 2019, Busan, Republic of Korea.

44. Mohan V, Mapari JA, Karnad PD, Mann JS, Maheshwari VK, et al. Reduced diabetes mellitus-related comorbidities by regular self-monitoring of blood glucose: economic and quality of life implications. Indian J Endocrinol Metab. 2018;22(4):461–5.

45. Moström P, Ahlén E, Imberg H, et al. Adherence of self-monitoring of blood glucose in persons with type 1 diabetes in Sweden. BMJ Open Diab Res Care. 2017;5:e000342.

46. Rossi MC, et al. Real-world use of self-monitoring of blood glucose in people with type 2 diabetes: an urgent need for improvement. Acta Diabetol. 2018;55:1059–66.

47. Tavares R, et al. Differences in self-monitored, blood glucose test strip utilization by therapy for type 2 diabetes mellitus. Acta Diabetol. 2016;53:483–92.

48. Farmer A, et al. Frequency of self-monitoring of blood glucose in patients with type 2 diabetes: association with hypoglycaemic events. Curr Med Res Opin. 2008;24:3097–104.

49. Lecomte P, et al. Self-monitoring of blood glucose in people with type 1 and type 2 diabetes living in France: the entered study 2001. Diabetes Metab. 2008;34:219–26.

50. Al-Keilani MS, et al. Self-monitoring of blood glucose among patients with diabetes in Jordan: perception, adherence, and influential factors. Diabetes Res Clin Pract. 2017;126:79–85.

51. Vincze G, et al. Factors associated with adherence to self-monitoring of blood glucose among persons with diabetes. Diabetes Educ. 2004;30(1):112–25.

52. Xin W, et al. Adherence to self-monitoring of blood glucose in Chinese patients with type 2 diabetes: current status and influential factors based on electronic questionnaires. Patient Prefer Adherence. 2019;13:1269–82.

53. Hu ZD, et al. Compliance to self-monitoring of blood glucose among patients with type 2 diabetes mellitus and its influential factors: a real-world cross-sectional study based on the Tencent TDF-I blood glucose monitoring platform. mHealth. 2017;3:25–30.

54. Stephani V, et al. Self-management of diabetes in Sub-Saharan Africa: a systematic review. BMC Public Health. 2018;18:1148–58.

55. International Diabetes Federation. D-Net, Diabetes Network for Health professionals. You can't manage what you can't measure, CGM or SMBG? 01 Oct 2019. https://d-net.idf.org/en/discussions/181-you-can-t-manage-what-you-can-t-measure-cgm-or-smbg.html. Accessed 01-Apr-2020.

Chapter 6
Importance of Structured Diabetes Education

The favorable clinical outcomes in people with diabetes rely on individuals' self-management of the condition in their daily life. Although in many cases some form of support is provided, people with diabetes do not have any direct supervisor in their daily routines, which emphasizes the importance of education to manage diabetes.

Diabetes education is a critical part of diabetes management and has to be offered to all people with diabetes. Its aim is to equip them with the required knowledge about diabetes, competencies to make stand-alone decision-making, and skills for self-management. Numerous studies have demonstrated that diabetes education could result in improved diabetes care, reduced hospitalizations, and is cost effective in the long-term [1–4].

It is recommended that diabetes education is delivered through standardized and culturally adjusted modules covering different aspects of the living with diabetes. Ideally, such standardization would be done at a national level, based on cultural specifics, available technologies, treatments, lifestyle patterns, and healthcare resources.

Template modules have already been recommended by relevant international authorities and could easily be adopted as a minimum standard for development of country-specific materials [5]. The use of already prepared modules is particularly important in developing countries having limited resources to develop diabetes education modules entirely on their own [5]. Standardized dissemination and evaluation of diabetes knowledge is often labeled as Structured Diabetes Education Program (SDEP).

Structured Diabetes Education Programs should include modules on training-the-trainer, role of diabetes educator and management of diabetes care team, psychosocial and behavioral approaches, and community awareness [5].

There should be modules that cover diagnosis, classification and presentation of diabetes, pathophysiology, self-management, diabetes medication and insulin therapy. Modules should also cover physical activity, nutrition therapy, short-term

© Springer Nature Switzerland AG 2021
I. Smokovski, *Managing Diabetes in Low Income Countries*,
https://doi.org/10.1007/978-3-030-51469-3_6

complications and emergencies, sick-days, long-term complications, oral and sexual health [5].

Additionally, modules for diabetes in children and adolescents, GDM, pregnancy in pre-existing diabetes, older people, and perioperative management should also be included [5]. The above structure of the SDEP curriculum proposed by IDF should be considered as a minimum and not as a comprehensive list of modules for use by developing countries.

Modules need to be nationally adjusted, culturally and socially tailored, and delivered in the most appropriate format. Digital media and online SDEPs have multiple benefits, especially for lower resource countries where many diabetes specialties are lacking. The internet has been widely available and online platforms have become a viable option for dissemination of SDEPs and evaluation of the diabetes knowledge in people with diabetes.

Duration of SDEPs has to be individualized, as it is not possible to deliver and absorb all the information in a couple of hours. In case of online SDEPs, the recipient could set the dynamics of absorbing information.

Another advantage of online SDEP is that it could be implemented with limited resources, as the accredited materials could be posted online, ending with a diabetes knowledge test. Healthcare providers should direct the person with diabetes towards the online program and will record the test result in the individual EHRs. Diabetes care team would be available for any questions or dilemmas the person might have during the course of SDEP.

Online SDEP becomes essential when people with diabetes are not able to leave their homes, as during the global pandemic with COVID-19. In those situations when people with diabetes are one of the most critical categories for morbidity and mortality, online platforms become the only communication channel for delivering SDEP. Even more, a complete physician's follow-up visit could be performed via telemedicine with the possibility to access individual EHRs and analyze reports derived from BGMs or CGMs.

It is critical that SDEP is completed not just with evaluation of knowledge and skills acquired by the people with diabetes, but also with their feedback on the content and delivery of SDEP. Only mutual assessment and feedback could lead to acquiring higher levels of education by people with diabetes, and improvement of SDEP content by the diabetes care team.

Furthermore, it is important how often and when to re-introduce SDEP in a particular person with diabetes, as single SDEP in a newly diagnosed, distressed and distracted people, is not expected to equip them with long-term knowledge. According to the ADA, there are four critical times for implementation or re-assessment of SDEP: at diagnosis, annually, when complicating factors arise, and when transitions in care occur [1].

It is obvious that SDEP has to be provided at the time of diagnosis, and due to the stress with the new situation, it would be beneficial if the person with diabetes is accompanied by another person from the inner circle, such as a spouse, partner, parent, child or a friend. The closest people to a person with diabetes have to be aware of all the aspects covered by the SDEP. They should, preferably, accompany the person with diabetes throughout the complete course of SDEP.

One example of the need to have an accompanying person during SDEP is when a spouse or a partner is more often preparing the meals, and has to be aware of the nutritional characteristics of various foods that might affect glycaemia. Another example is the need to educate the people from inner circle on the signs and symptoms of hypoglycemia, a common acute diabetes complication in people with diabetes. Unfortunately, according to the IDF estimates, less than 50% of people with diabetes and 25% of family members of people with diabetes have access to diabetes education programs (Fig. 6.1) [6].

Continuous, documented SDEP has to be performed at least on an annual basis with recording of individuals' success to acquire the necessary knowledge, skills and competencies. The capturing of individuals' achievements after SDEP completion would enable continuous monitoring of a person's knowledge, similar to monitoring of parameters for metabolic control. When complicating factors or transition in care occurs, the SDEP needs to be re-introduced, regardless of the time elapsed since the previous diabetes education [1].

It is crucial for the healthcare system in developing countries to understand and acknowledge the importance of the SDEP. In many cases the SDEP has not been implemented as recommended, although the other components of diabetes management (staff, medication, glucose monitoring) have been available. Structured

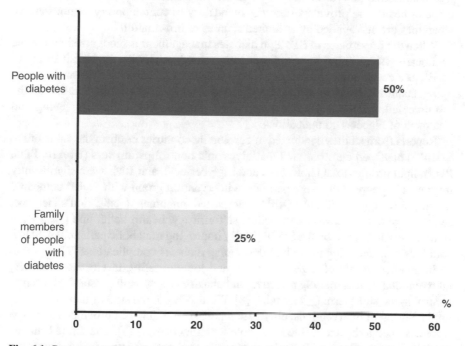

Fig. 6.1 Percentage of people with diabetes and their family members with access to diabetes education programs, data adapted from Ref. [6]

diabetes education should be focused on the needs, clinical outcomes, overall health and well-being of the person with diabetes, and should be considered at every physician's visit.

The way SDEP is offered may be different: could be in individual settings, group settings, or combined—certain modules could be covered individually, and others in groups. It is preferred that education programs involve the members of the whole diabetes care team. It would be beneficial if peer-to-peer dissemination of information is also included as part of the SDEP, conveyed by other people with diabetes, particularly for people with type 1 diabetes. The importance of such peer-to-peer communication is often exceeding the one delivered through the standardized modules of SDEP. It is crucial that such communication is provided in a controlled and approved manner.

In the era of digital technologies, it is impossible to prevent people from encountering numerous unverified and often harmful diabetes related information, especially through the social media. Misleading information in many cases offers magical solutions, frequently resulting in devastating consequences in the form of acute diabetes complications. It is difficult to assess the long-term deleterious effects such spread of false information might have on the development of chronic diabetes complications.

People with diabetes from developing, less regulated countries, are more prone to be exposed to non-medical schemes for diabetes management. Providing them with knowledge how to identify the risk and to immediately discuss it with their diabetes healthcare providers becomes mandatory in contemporary circumstances, when they are surrounded by unlimited sources of information.

When the importance of SDEP in diabetes management is recognized within the healthcare system, it has to be appropriately valued; otherwise the sustainability of SDEP as a continuous process would be jeopardized. Healthcare systems in developing countries have to allocate dedicated resources for SDEP, similar to the resources allocated for glucose monitoring, diabetes medication, screening and treatment of diabetes complications.

Reports from studies conducted in developing countries confirm the value of the SDEP. It has been demonstrated that glycaemic control parameters (HbA1c, FPG, PPG), lipid profile (total cholesterol and triglycerides), and BMI were significantly improved in people who were part of the intervention group with SDEP, compared to the control group without SDEP [7]. Reported outcomes (medication adherence, self-management behavior, knowledge, self-efficacy, health belief and QoL) were significantly improved by the SDEP [7]. By improving metabolic parameters, SDEP could result in reducing the risk of developing diabetes complications [7].

In another review of SDEPs in high- and low-mortality developing countries, interventions were generally effective on behavior change and persons' glycaemic control in the short term (≤ 9 months) [8]. While 57% of the studies mentioned cultural tailoring of interventions, only 17% reported on training of providers, and 39% were designed to be accessible for people with low literacy [8]. The limited studies available suggest that SDEPs in developing countries are effective in the short term, but must be tailored to conform to the cultural aspects of the target population [8].

Studies of SDEPs in developing countries from Sub-Saharan Africa also confirmed the importance of education in people with diabetes. Combination of weekly group educational sessions on nutritional aspects with monthly follow up sessions significantly reduced the intake of energy and starchy food [9]. Another study with weekly contacts over a period of four months significantly improved the healthy eating habits of people with diabetes [10].

Group education programs about self-care behaviors in developing countries improved the foot care of participants [11, 12]. In addition, four one-hour group education sessions on nutritional aspects significantly increased the level of adherence [11, 12].

Education levels are lower in most of the developing countries and the channels of communication are limited. It is a challenge to convey the information to people with diabetes in low-income countries if there is a limited access to healthcare, education, mass media or online platforms.

Despite the studies above, SDEPs in most developing countries are limited in scope, content and consistency, and it is largely unknown how people from developing countries utilize the SDEP for managing their diabetes [13, 14].

Structured Diabetes Education Programs should become a mandatory part of the National Diabetes Care guidelines in developing countries. It needs to be stipulated in the guidelines that every person with diabetes has to be offered SDEP, followed by testing of acquired diabetes knowledge, skills and competencies [15]. In addition, National Diabetes Care guidelines in developing countries should potentiate that people with diabetes need to be informed about the importance of SDEP as an integral part of their diabetes management [15].

Although numerous diabetes care initiatives running in developing countries were acknowledged by relevant international authorities, it was also recognized that many SDEP recommendations were not fully implemented, and significant number of people with both type 1 and type 2 diabetes were not offered SDEPs, neither at the time of diagnosis nor later during the course of the disease [16].

Despite the need for improved education of people with diabetes, there is also a need for improved education of the physicians treating diabetes, as reported from a study conducted in developing countries [17]. Physicians need to be aware of the current guidelines in order to provide proper diabetes care. Many physicians noted adequate glycaemic control despite non availability of HbA1c measurements, whereas others overestimated the proportions of people at goal [17]. In addition, the clinical inertia of delayed intensification of therapy was reported among physicians [17].

The IDF estimates that currently 20% of healthcare professionals do not receive any postgraduate training in diabetes [6]. It once again stresses the need of education not only towards the people with diabetes and their family members, but also towards the healthcare professionals.

It is critical who is delivering the diabetes education for healthcare providers, as it is very important that those sources are unbiased and financed with unrestricted grants. One of the most important channels of exerting influence on prescribing patterns of physicians is through medical education. Many of those medical education events or resources in developing countries are not evidence based and balanced, and are favoring particular treatment sponsored by certain pharmaceutical company. This could significantly drive the costs of diabetes treatment higher, as explained in the previous chapters.

Furthermore, SDEPs in developing countries are mainly available in diabetes care facilities in larger cities, and a lack of resources was recognized as a reason for the paucity in diabetes education in developing countries [17]. It was mentioned that diabetes prevalence has been higher in rural compared to urban areas in the Republic of North Macedonia [18].

One of the possible explanations for this surprising finding could be the limited access to adequate SDEP in rural areas due to the lack of Diabetes Centers [18]. Diabetes Centers are not only providing care for people diagnosed with diabetes, but are also managing people with prediabetes. It was therefore recognized that lack of those centers in rural areas could be a reason for the higher diabetes prevalence in rural compared to urban population [18].

There have been no studies so far comparing the effect of SDEP on the level of diabetes knowledge and metabolic control in insulin-treated people, if SDEP is provided at the time of diagnosis or later during the course of diabetes [19].

Such study comparing the diabetes knowledge between insulin-treated people with diabetes offered SDEP at the time of diagnosis with those offered unstructured education, and evaluating the effects of the SDEP on their diabetes knowledge immediately after, and 1 year after completion, has been reported from the Republic of North Macedonia [19]. In addition, glycaemic control was compared in both groups at baseline, and one year after SDEP [19].

Insulin treated people with diabetes demonstrated inadequate diabetes knowledge and there was no difference in the previously acquired knowledge between the groups, regardless if people were offered SDEP or unstructured education at the time of diagnosis [19], Such findings at baseline demonstrate the need to implement the National Diabetes Care guidelines' recommendations and offer SDEP at least annually with test of the acquired diabetes knowledge [15]. Despite SDEP being delivered at the time of diagnosis, if it is not repeated at least annually, the benefits are lost when compared to unstructured education.

As anticipated, diabetes knowledge was significantly improved in both groups after 5 days of SDEP, and both groups passed the predefined threshold of knowledge test with no between-group differences in the test results [19].

When the same diabetes knowledge test was taken after 1 year, lower results were observed in both groups, if compared to the results obtained after the completion of SDEP [19]. Nonetheless, these results were significantly higher than those obtained before the SDEP, indicating sustainable effect of SDEP after 1 year [19]. Both groups demonstrated adequate diabetes knowledge 1 year after SDEP by passing the predefined threshold [19].

In addition, lower HbA1c values were measured in both groups after 1 year, with no between-group difference in HbA1c reduction. The improved glycaemic control could be attributed to the increase in diabetes knowledge after 1 year; however, even the reduced values of HbA1c were well above the recommended targets [1, 15, 19].

The inadequate glycaemic control achieved 1 year after SDEP supports the recommendations from the National Diabetes Care guidelines to repeat the education and testing of diabetes knowledge at least annually [15, 19]. Improvement of glycaemic control after SDEP and the positive effects of SDEP on diabetes knowledge have been reported from similar studies in developed countries [20–24].

It would be of interest to further evaluate the sustainable effects of SDEP on diabetes knowledge and metabolic control for a period longer than 1 year, and to establish the optimal frequency and content of SDEP for each person.

Structured diabetes education should be appropriate in terms of cultural, linguistic needs or level of literacy. Adequate resources need to be secured for the diabetes educators, who should be qualified, competent and adequately trained. As part of the patient-centric healthcare system, people should also be encouraged to take an active role in the creation and implementation of SDEPs.

Healthcare providers need to be cautious when educating people with diabetes how to use and interpret results from the BGMs. It should be considered that many people in developing countries are of advanced age, have a lower level of education, and are not familiar with English, the standard language of messages and alerts on the BGM display. The education on SMBG has to be adjusted to the level of education of the people who would use it. Situations are common when people with diabetes are looking at the display upside down reading 14 mmol/L (252 mg/dL) instead of 'hi', a dangerous situation of hyperglycemia that may result in DKA or HHS (Fig. 6.2) [25].

Another example of misreading the BGM display by an older person not familiar with English is when 'lo' (low) was read as 10 mmol/L (180 mg/dL), and hypoglycemia requiring treatment was misinterpreted (Fig. 6.2) [25]. People with diabetes should be evaluated for obtaining an acceptable level of knowledge and skills before using the BGMs on their own.

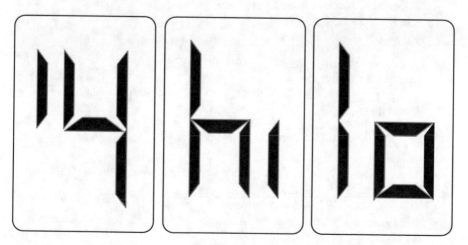

Fig. 6.2 Pitfalls in reading the display of BGMs [25]. BGMs Blood Glucose Meters

According to the IDF, one of the challenges developing countries face is addressing the lack of time and shortages of personnel to offer diabetes education [16]. Diet counseling in people with type 2 diabetes is generally provided by diabetes nurses concentrated in urban areas and limited to people on insulin. Dietitians are not involved in diabetes treatment in most of the developing countries. Physicians' education in developing countries includes very little practical instruction on the role of nutrition in disease prevention or treatment. Furthermore, there is a shortage of registered nurses with training in diabetes [16].

Majority of population with diabetes in developing countries is lacking access to healthcare providers involved in SDEP. Offering continuous and high-quality SDEP has been a challenge even for the developed countries, which only suggests the magnitude of the problem for the developing countries.

Novel digital technologies have to be used to enforce SDEP and such initiatives might be of particular interest for developing countries. It has been acknowledged that mobile technologies, such as mobile banking, are penetrating fast even in the less developed countries. As internet and mobile technologies become widely available, online or m-Health based SDEP modules could be a cost-effective solution.

The essence of SDEP is re-education and re-evaluation. Platforms with records of scores the person achieves after SDEP would be valuable information for the healthcare provider. Additionally, it would be of great benefit if such scores are captured in the individual EHRs, together with the other diabetes related information that need to be continuously monitored.

Continuous SDEP results in a sustainable increase of diabetes knowledge attained by people with diabetes, and could ultimately lead to improved glycaemic control and reduced risk of diabetes complications.

What needs to be done for implementation of structured diabetes education programs in developing countries?
Each developing country should…

- …include SDEP as a key activity of diabetes management in the National Diabetes Care guidelines,
- …offer SDEP through standardized, culturally adjusted modules, covering different aspects of the living with diabetes;
- …offer SDEP to people with diabetes minimum at the four critical times: at diagnosis, annually, when complicating factors arise, and when transitions in care occur;
- … ensure test scores after completion of SDEP are recorded in individual EHRs as part of the NeHS;
- …allocate resources for SDEP to ensure its sustainability,
- …consider online SDEP and m-Health solutions in a setting of limited resources.

References

1. American Diabetes Association. Standards of medical care in diabetes 2020. Diabetes Care. 2020;43(1):s1–212.
2. Balamurugan A, Ohsfeldt R, Hughes T, Phillips M. Diabetes self-management education program for Medicaid recipients: a continuous quality improvement process. Diabetes Educ. 2006;32:893–900.
3. North SL, Palmer GA. Outcome analysis of hemoglobin A1c, weight, and blood pressure in a VA diabetes education program. J Nutr Educ Behav. 2015;47:28–35.
4. Boren SA, Fitzner KA, Panhalkar PS, Specker JE. Costs and benefits associated with diabetes education: a review of the literature. Diabetes Educ. 2009;35:72–96.
5. International Diabetes Federation. Consultative section on diabetes education. International Curriculum for Diabetes Health Professional Education, 2008.
6. International Diabetes Federation. IDF schools of diabetes. https://idf.org/our-activities/education/idf-school-of-diabetes.html.Accessed 01-Apr-2020.
7. Mikhael ME, Hassali AM, Hussain AS. Effectiveness of diabetes self-management educational programs for type 2 diabetes mellitus patients in Middle East countries: a systematic review. Diabetes Metab Syndr Obes. 2020;13:117–38.
8. Dube L, Van den Broucke S, Housiaux M. Type 2 diabetes self-management education programs in high and low mortality developing countries: a systematic review. Diabetes Educ. 2014; https://doi.org/10.1177/0145721714558305.
9. Muchiri JW, Gericke GJ, Rheeder P. Effect of a nutrition education programme on clinical status and dietary behaviours of adults with type 2 diabetes in a resource-limited setting in South Africa: a randomised controlled trial. Public Health Nutr. 2016;19(1):142–55.
10. Baumann LC, Frederick N, Betty N, Jospehine E, Agatha N. A demonstration of peer support for Ugandan adults with type 2 diabetes. Int J Behav Med. 2015;22(3):374–83.
11. van der Does AM, Mash R. Evaluation of the "take five school": an education programme for people with type 2 diabetes in the Western cape, South Africa. Prim Care Diab. 2013;7(4):289–95.
12. Mash B, Levitt N, Steyn K, Zwarenstein M, Rollnick S. Effectiveness of a group diabetes education programme in underserved communities in South Africa: pragmatic cluster randomized control trial. BMC Fam Pract. 2012;13:126.
13. Rawal LB, Tapp RJ, Williams ED, Chan C, Yasin S, Oldenburg B. Prevention of type 2 diabetes and its complications in developing countries: a review. Int J Behav Med. 2012;19(2):121–33.
14. Dube L, Van den Broucke S, Dhoore W, Kalweit K, Housiaux M. An audit of diabetes self-management education programs in South Africa. J Public Health Res. 2015;4(3):581. https://doi.org/10.4081/jphr.2015.581.
15. Ministry of Health. Guideline on healthcare related to the treatment and control of type 2 diabetes. Off J Repub Macedonia. 2015;40:15–34.
16. International Diabetes Federation. Diabetes in Europe policy puzzle. The State We Are In. 4th ed. Brussels, Belgium: International Diabetes Federation; 2014.
17. Chan CHJ, Gagliardino JJ, Baik HS, Chantelot JM, Ferreira RGS, et al. on behalf of IDPMS Investigators. Multifaceted determinants for achieving glycemic control the International Diabetes Management Practice Study (IDMPS). Diabetes Care 2009; 32:227–233.
18. Smokovski I, Milenkovic T, Cho HN. First stratified diabetes prevalence data for Republic of Macedonia derived from the National e-Health System. Diabetes Res Clin Pract. 2018;143:179–83.
19. Milenkovic T, Smokovski I, Bozhinovska N, Rahelic D, Misevska JS, et al. Effects of structured diabetes education program on diabetes knowledge and metabolic control in insulin-treated diabetes patients from the Republic of Macedonia. Endocr Oncol Metab. 2017; https://doi.org/10.21040/eom/2017.3.1.1.

20. Ko SH, Song KH, Kim SR, Lee JM, Kim JS, et al. Long-term effects of a structured intensive diabetes education programme (SIDEP) in patients with Type 2 diabetes mellitus – a 4-year follow-up study. Diabet Med. 2007;24:55–62.
21. Deakin TA, Cade JE, Williams R, Greenwood DC. Structured patient education: The diabetes X-PERT Programme makes a difference. Diabet Med. 2006;23:944–54.
22. Speight J, Holmes-Truscott E, Harvey DM, Hendrieckx C, Hagger VL, et al. Structured Type 1 diabetes education delivered in routine care in Australia reduces diabetes-related emergencies and severe diabetes-related distress: the OzDAFNE program. Diabetes Res Clin Pract. 2016;112:65–72.
23. Pieber TR, Brunner GA, Schnedl WJ, Schattenberg S, Kaufmann P, et al. Evaluation of a structured outpatient group education program for intensive insulin therapy. Diabetes Care. 1995;18:625–30.
24. Khunti K, Gray LJ, Skinner T, Carey ME, Realf K, Dallosso H, et al. Effectiveness of diabetes education and self-management program (DESMOND) for people with newly diagnosed Type 2 diabetes mellitus: three year follow-up of a cluster randomized controlled trial in primary care. BMJ. 2012;344:e2333. https://doi.org/10.1136/bmj.e2333.
25. Smokovski I. Self-monitoring as an important tool in preventing diabetes complications – evidence from the real world. International Diabetes Federation Congress, 02–06 Dec 2019, Busan, Republic of Korea.

Chapter 7
Benefits of Centralized e-Health System in Diabetes Care

We are living in a paperless, digital age, and EHRs are becoming the standard of capturing patient related information. Understandably, the penetration of EHR systems is higher in developed compared to developing countries. Use of EHRs facilitates healthcare provider decisions resulting in better clinical care and improved patient outcomes.

Importance of introducing EHR in developing countries has been emphasized by the WHO almost 15 years ago, when the EHR Manual for developing countries was published [1]. Inadequate health information systems have been identified as a major challenge in the healthcare systems of many developing countries, and EHRs have not been widely implemented in those countries [1, 2].

Some of the reasons identified for inadequate use of EHRs in developing countries have been the high costs of procurement and maintenance of the EHR systems, lack of financial incentives and priorities, and inadequate internet connectivity [3].

It is important for lower resource countries to consider development of their own, national EHRs, instead of procuring global, costly EHR solutions. For that purpose they could use the expertise of other developing countries that are more advanced in the implementation of EHR. Such in-house solutions could be based on the open standards and open source software [4].

However, it is not enough just to have an EHR system capturing the medical information, including diabetes care parameters. The critical part of implementing EHR systems is to make them communicate with each other and provide interoperability, in order to share patient related information across the country. It is important that wherever the patient goes within a country, the healthcare providers have access to the patient's medical history.

It is true nowadays that in most developed countries, such as the US, Germany or Sweden, patient related information is captured electronically in sophisticated EHR systems. However, interoperability of EHR systems is inadequate even in those developed countries, as the systems are not exchanging patient information with each other. It is great to have EHR systems, but if the records could not be easily

© Springer Nature Switzerland AG 2021
I. Smokovski, *Managing Diabetes in Low Income Countries*,
https://doi.org/10.1007/978-3-030-51469-3_7

accessed by all the providers who need them and the patients themselves, then there is a lack of benefit of using such systems.

This is also relevant for the diabetes related information captured in EHRs of the most developed countries, if different systems are used in different hospitals. Hence, if a person with diabetes goes from one city or region to another within the same country, the healthcare providers would know nothing about its diabetes.

One striking example of a disastrous outcome due to non-integration of EHRs, even in the most developed healthcare systems such as Germany, was the case of Germanwings pilot Andreas Lubitz. He was unable to sleep because of what he believed were vision problems, and had consulted numerous doctors fearing he was going blind. Andreas Lubitz was taking prescription medicines and suffered from a psychosomatic illness, treated for suicidal tendencies, and was declared unfit to work by doctors, and absolutely unfit to operate an aircraft.

Andreas Lubitz should have never been allowed to be in control of an airplane. Nevertheless, medical secrecy requirements prevented above information to be available to Germanwings, and the doctors were not aware of the medical records of other doctors due to a missing interoperability of the different EHRs. It all ended up in catastrophe when Andreas Lubitz took over the control of Germanwings flight number 9525 from Barcelona to Dusseldorf, deliberately causing a crash on 24-March-2015, and killing all 144 passengers onboard. If the EHR systems of all the doctors he visited had been integrated, this tragedy could have probably been prevented.

Integration of the EHR systems should not only be between hospitals, but also between all relevant stakeholders across all layers of healthcare. All healthcare entities have to be integrated in a centralized, National e-Health System. Diabetes related information has to be a substantial part of the NeHS. In addition to improving the clinical care and patient outcomes, a centralized, integrated EHR system could serve as a database for healthcare authorities to perform numerous analyses at a national level, thus enabling the adequate management of medical conditions and available resources.

Although there are outstanding national registers in developed countries for certain conditions; the EHR systems in the majority of those countries are not centrally integrated. It is interesting that what is non-existent in the most developed countries is available in a developing, low-resource country, such as the Republic of North Macedonia. Accordingly, if it could have been implemented in a country like the Republic of North Macedonia, it would be possible to implement it in any developing country with limited resources.

Introduction of NeHS in the Republic of North Macedonia on 01-July-2013 was a revolutionary step in monitoring and improving the performance of national healthcare system. It was a domestically developed platform, created and tailored according to the instructions from the Ministry of Health. The comprehensive, national EHR system covered all citizens across the three healthcare levels: primary care provided by family physicians, secondary care provided by specialists in general and regional hospitals, and tertiary care provided by university clinics. Implementation of the NeHS has been praised internationally as a key platform for improving the performance of the national healthcare system [5–7].

It is worth noting that the NeHS was domestically developed and the costs for development and maintenance have been a fraction of the costs of similar comprehensive, global e-Health solutions on the market. A dedicated Directorate for e-Health was formed within the Ministry of Health, responsible for maintaining and upgrading the NeHS, and reporting directly to the Minister of Health. The Directorate for e-Health has been closely cooperating with the healthcare authorities and the Institute of Public Health, as it has become possible to instantly generate and analyze numerous public healthcare data.

European Healthcare Consumer Index (EHCI) Report for 2014 stated that the Republic of North Macedonia has made the most remarkable advance in the EHCI scoring of any country in the history of the Index, from 27th to 16th place, largely due to eliminating waiting lists by implementing the real time e-Booking system (Fig. 7.1) [5–9].

The value of centralized, integrated EHR systems goes beyond the online appointments that have largely facilitated healthcare access for patients, including those with diabetes. It has been an online, cloud-based platform for EHRs of the entire population in the Republic of North Macedonia [5, 6, 8, 9]. Other countries have also expressed interest in providing the whole or elements of the NeHS in their national healthcare systems.

Since the beginning of 2015, the diabetes care module in the NeHS was upgraded with the possibility to record diabetes treatment, metabolic parameters and diabetes

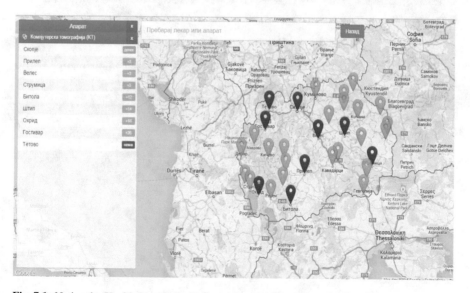

Fig. 7.1 National e-Health System in the Republic of North Macedonia [5–9]

complications (Fig. 7.2a, b) [5–9]. In that way, the NeHS has provided endless possibilities for monitoring prevalence of morbidities and mortalities, prescribed medications, referrals across the system, metabolic control, and numerous other analyses in one of the worst hit populations in Europe [5–9].

Integration of diabetes related data in NeHS was one of the initiatives undertaken to manage the burden of diabetes in the Republic of North Macedonia (Fig. 7.3) [9–11]. Other initiatives included designating diabetes mellitus as a specific medical condition in the Law on Healthcare; adopting international guidelines as National Diabetes Care guidelines published in the Official Journal of Republic of North Macedonia, where laws are published, further emphasizing the importance of diabetes as a nationwide condition (Fig. 7.3) [9–11]. The National Diabetes Register was also created within the NeHS containing more detailed information about the people with diabetes (Fig. 7.3) [9–11].

Additional initiatives included formation of National Diabetes Committee according to the Law on Healthcare (Fig. 7.3) [9–11]. The National Diabetes Committee has been responsible for the development of National Diabetes Plan, implementation of the National Diabetes Care guidelines and monitoring of adherence to the guidelines.

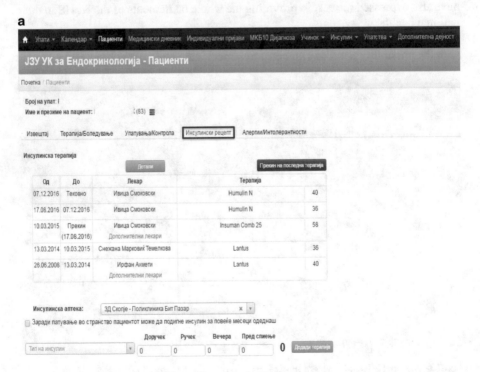

Fig. 7.2 Integration of diabetes related data in NeHS (**a**) diabetes treatment (**b**) metabolic parameters and diabetes complications [5–9]

b

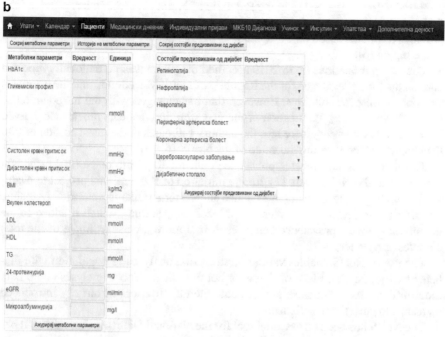

Fig. 7.2 (continued)

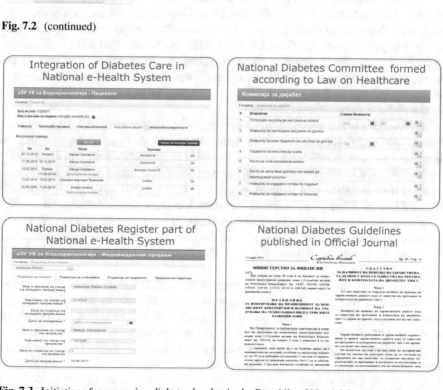

Fig. 7.3 Initiatives for managing diabetes burden in the Republic of North Macedonia [9–11]

Introduction of the NeHS in the Republic of North Macedonia has provided the first opportunity to evaluate the prevalence of diagnosed diabetes cases, unlike the previous estimates based on extrapolations of high quality data from other countries in the region [6].

The IDF publications up to 2019 specified that there was no nationally reported data on the total prevalence for the Republic of North Macedonia, and the estimates were based on extrapolations. However, that has changed with the introduction of the NeHS [6, 12, 13]. Publication of the first stratified diabetes prevalence derived from the NeHS was considered for the country estimates in the latest edition of IDF Diabetes Atlas, confirming the value of the NeHS [6, 13].

The first stratified diabetes prevalence data for Republic of North Macedonia derived from the NeHS were key for the initiation of IDF regional project to evaluate the undiagnosed diabetes prevalence in Western Balkans countries (Albania, Bosnia and Herzegovina, Montenegro, Macedonia, Serbia), which if added to the diagnosed diabetes prevalence could result in a more precise estimate of the total diabetes prevalence.

The use of NeHS enables various stratification analyses in population with diabetes by age, gender, place of living, or comorbidities. Those analyses could help monitor diabetes prevalence, and evaluate the effectiveness of already introduced measures to curb the prevalence.

The NeHS has been an essential tool for the National Diabetes Committee. It has served as a platform for rationalization of diabetes treatment by monitoring prescribers' adherence to the guidelines, thus being critical in managing the exponentially rising diabetes costs. Thanks to the NeHS, prescribers who were violating the guidelines were identified which played a crucial role in the rationalization of insulin treatment costs by almost 50% in 4 years, despite the cumulative annual growth of insulin volume by 5%, seven-fold increase in the free test strips, and introduction of novel diabetes treatment classes.

The NeHS has also served as a human resources management tool. Its use identified if additional human resources were needed in diabetes care, resulting in increased number of residencies and fellowships in Endocrinology and Diabetes.

Its value as a human resources tool has been critical as many physicians from the country have left their jobs in the Republic of North Macedonia, and moved to better paid jobs in developed European countries, leaving a gap in the national system. The migration of physicians is a huge problem for the other developing countries, as well. The problem is more complex as the ones who migrate are predominantly younger specialists and fellows, leaving the domestic system with the ageing physicians' population.

By analyzing the workload of the remaining providers from the NeHS, such as the number of patients, visits, referrals, complexity of patients and other engagements of the providers, it was possible to reallocate the remaining resources or redistribute the workload to provide an adequate diabetes care.

Analysis of geographical distribution of diabetes population from the NeHS resulted in decisions to open additional Diabetes Centers and insulin pharmacies at locations where those were missing. As a result, in less than 2 years, 3 more Diabetes

Centers and insulin pharmacies were opened in the country, adding to the total number of 41 Diabetes Centers nationwide.

Furthermore, NeHS has become an essential platform for Predictive, Preventive
and Personalized Medicine (PPPM) in people with diabetes. The concept of PPPM
has emerged as the focal point of efforts in healthcare aimed at controlling the prevalence and management of NCDs, including diabetes [14–17].

The NeHS has been used as a platform for Predictive Diabetes Care, as it has
enabled monitoring of metabolic control parameters and the associated predicted
risk for diabetes complications. The NeHS could be used for monitoring of predicted diabetes risk and identifying high risk individuals for developing diabetes.

The NeHS has been a platform for Preventive Diabetes Care, as it has enabled
monitoring of diabetes complications, and provides directions for preventive activities to avoid or delay diabetes complications. It also provides monitoring of modifiable risk factors for prevention of diabetes.

Finally, the NeHS has served as a platform for Personalized Diabetes Care, providing diabetes care based on individual glycaemic control and comorbidities. The
NeHS data are available to care-givers across all healthcare levels and there is a
potential of adding new scientifically sound and approved biomarkers to further
personalize diabetes care in the future.

Taking into consideration that diabetes has been a huge healthcare and socioeconomic burden for the country, the analysis of data on metabolic control in people
with diabetes has been of utmost importance. A study was performed to analyze the
metabolic control in insulin treated people with diabetes from the Republic of North
Macedonia [18].

National e-Health System was searched for all insulin-treated people with data in
their EHRs on any of the metabolic parameters. Analysis of the NeHS found that the
insulin-treated people with diabetes in the Republic of North Macedonia had mean
HbA1c of 7.8 ± 1.8%. It was found that 37.8% of the people with diabetes achieved
target HbA1c ≤ 7%; whereas 25.9% had HbA1c >7% and ≤8%; and 36.3% had
HbA1c >8% (Fig. 7.4) [18].

First metabolic control results in insulin-treated people with diabetes derived
from the NeHS have reported that there is a need for improvement of glycaemic
control, as 36.3% of subjects had poor glycaemic control (HbA1c > 8%)
(Fig. 7.4) [18].

In addition, the need for improvement of weight management was identified, as
mean BMI was 30.4 ± 5.2 kg/m² [18]. The need for improvement of lipid management was also reported as more than half of the subjects had total cholesterol and
LDL above the recommended targets [18, 19]. Analysis discovered that only 16.8%
of subjects had any metabolic data in their EHRs, so change from optional to mandatory recording of metabolic parameters was suggested as necessary to improve
the individual and national metabolic control [18, 19].

If we compare the results of glycaemic control in the Republic of North Macedonia,
where 37.8% of the people with diabetes were on target, with the glycaemic control
from developed European countries, we could find it comparable to Italy (36% of
cases on target), and the UK (39% of cases on target), whereas other developed

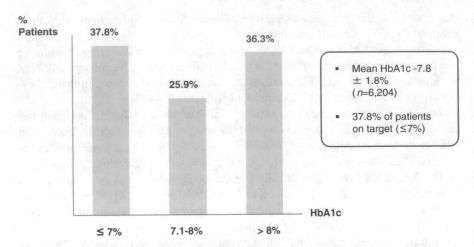

Fig. 7.4 Glycaemic control in insulin-treated people with diabetes derived from the NeHS [18]

countries had better glycaemic control, including the Netherlands (71%), France (65%), Belgium (60%), Sweden (57%), Ireland (53%), and Germany (49%) [18, 20].

It is interesting that the study in the developed European countries was also conducted by using EHRs and it covered a total of 7,597 subjects from 8 developed European countries, compared to the study from NeHS in the small country of Republic of North Macedonia which analyzed 6,204 individuals, only confirming the power of centralized, integrated e-Health systems [18, 20].

Another interesting observation is that despite the reduction of penetration of insulin analogues, the achieved glycaemic control was comparable with some of the developed European countries, and improved compared to previous reports of glycaemic control in the country [21, 22].

The NeHS could also provide information on the percentage of people with diabetes achieving metabolic targets at the level of region, city, healthcare institution, or individual physician. In that way, it is possible to create benchmarks and identify the best and worst performers. Improvements in achieving targets at the physicians' level contribute to the better national metabolic control. Those metrics could be defined for various processes, including achieving metabolic control, screening for complications, or cost-effective use of diabetes treatments. Institutions and physicians have to be incentivized to achieve better performance.

The NeHS was also used to evaluate the use of metformin in people with type 2 diabetes in the country. Surprisingly, it was found that metformin was not adequately titrated and the majority of people with diabetes were receiving suboptimal metformin doses. Similarly, it was identified that many patients were not receiving statin treatment for CVD prevention, although they were eligible for such treatment according to the National Diabetes Care guidelines.

It was already mentioned that Republic of North Macedonia is estimated to have one of the highest diabetes age-adjusted comparative prevalence in Europe, and is categorized as a very high risk country for CVD mortality, defined as CVD mortality >450/100,000 for men, and >350/100,000 for women [5, 6, 23].

By using the NeHS, for the first time it was possible to report the national prevalence of heart failure in people with type 2 diabetes in the Republic of North Macedonia, and their access to reimbursed treatment with SGLT2i or GLP-1RA after the initial treatment with metformin [24].

The national prevalence of heart failure in people with type 2 diabetes was found to be 12.0% [24]. Majority of the people with type 2 diabetes and heart failure were at the age of 60 years or above (92.5%) [24]. Only 0.5% of all people with type 2 diabetes and heart failure had access to fully reimbursed treatment with GLP-1RA or SGLT2i [24].

The first results of national prevalence of heart failure in people with type 2 diabetes derived from the NeHS suggested that despite the recent increase in the number of individuals with fully reimbursed treatment of SGLT2i or GLP-1RA, their access to those medications has still been very limited [24].

The access to NeHS is currently authorized only for various groups of healthcare providers with different rights. For example, physicians have full access, while nurses have limited access to the patient data. Citizens of the Republic of North Macedonia currently do not have access to their own EHRs, although such access has been enabled in certain developed countries. The next step should be to enable all citizens to have direct access to their own EHR data.

As we are moving from desktop to handheld devices, the next step in the improvement of NeHS would be to provide user friendly m-Health solution, or mobile app based platform. Such m-Health solutions are expected to have all the above mentioned functionalities, completely replacing the need of any paper documents in the healthcare processes.

It is interesting that developing countries might have an advantage in implementation of national, integrated EHR systems. Although it sounds paradoxical, many developed countries have EHR systems of different age and technology that are difficult to integrate on a national level. On the other hand, many developing countries are mainly EHR-naive, thus making the introduction of national, centralized, integrated systems much easier to implement. One such example has been the Republic of North Macedonia. But the explosion of mobile banking even in the less developed countries, reminds us that many other countries could easily benefit from the EHR systems as part of the m-Health solutions.

It would be beneficial if EHRs contain information on BMI, smoking status, and test score after SDEP; but also on physical activity, calories intake, and any novel biomarkers that might occur in the future. Individual EHRs could also include information from the glucose monitoring devices, such as BGMs and CGMs.

The NeHS could be used for monitoring the progression of subjects from prediabetes to type 2 diabetes. It could identify the people with prediabetes to focus preventive activities in this population. The NeHS could be used for monitoring of diabetes risk in people not diagnosed with diabetes.

The use of EHRs from NeHS has been crucial in performing telemedicine visits of people with diabetes in a time of a global infectious pandemic, such as the recent one with COVID-19. People with diabetes, as a high risk population for increased morbidity and mortality, have been strongly advised not to leave their homes. The role of telemedicine and NeHS in diabetes care will only increase in the future.

The NeHS has been valuable in times of natural disasters such as the floods in rural areas close to Skopje in 2016 when the people were stranded in their homes. The NeHS helped identify the people with diabetes in the affected area to facilitate the delivery of their medication.

It has to be considered that centralized, integrated e-Health systems would also be a target for breaching cyber security, exposing vital personal data from the medical histories. Efforts have to be made to protect the NeHS from data breaches through cyber-attacks.

The NeHS remains a key platform supporting the National Diabetes Committee activities in its main mission of improving glycaemic control in people with diabetes by adhering to National Diabetes Care guidelines, while preserving the sustainability of the health care system.

Finally, it needs to be mentioned that implementation of centralized, integrated NeHS in a developing country is not a smooth exercise. It has been met with strong resistance in the Republic of North Macedonia, since, suddenly, all the activities, workload and achievements of every physician, became very transparent.

However, the strong gains from the implementation of the NeHS justify the efforts to overcome all barriers that might appear on the way. In order to be successfully implemented, the NeHS requires strong political leadership and support from the medical community.

What could be the benefits from a centralized e-Health System in Diabetes Care?

Each developing country should…

- …have NeHS as a critical tool for Predictive, Preventive and Personalized diabetes care;
- …enable NeHS to include data on dietary pattern, physical activity, diabetes education, in addition to metabolic parameters in EHRs of people with diabetes;
- …consider integration of BGM and CGM data into the NeHS;
- …use analysis from the NeHS as a cornerstone for the national diabetes care policies;
- …provide its citizens with access to their own EHRs.

References

1. World Health Organization. Electronic Health Records – Manual for Developing Countries, 2006.
2. Sikhondze CN, Erasmus L. Electronic medical records: a developing and developed country analysis. Int Assoc Manag Technol Conf Proc. 2016:273–90.
3. Odekunle FF, Odekunle OR, Shankar S. Why sub-Saharan Africa lags in electronic health record adoption and possible strategies to increase its adoption in this region. Int J Health Sci (Qassim). 2017;11(4):59–64.

4. Fraser H, Biondich P, Moodley D, Choi S, Mamlin WB, et al. Implementing electronic medical record systems in developing countries. Inform Prim Care. 2005;13:83–95.
5. Smokovski I, Milenkovic T, Trapp C, Mitov A. Diabetes care in the Republic of Macedonia: challenges and opportunities. Ann Global Health. 2015;81(6):792–802.
6. Smokovski I, Milenkovic T, Cho HN. First stratified diabetes prevalence data for Republic of Macedonia derived from the National eHealth System. Diabetes Res Clin Pract. 2018;143:179–83.
7. Health Consumer Powerhouse. Euro health consumer index report, 2014. Taby, Sweden: Health Consumer Powerhouse. 2015. https://healthpowerhouse.com/media/EHCI-2014/EHCI-2014-report.pdf. Accessed 20 March 2020.
8. Velinov G, Jakimovski B, Lesovski D, Ivanova Panova D, Frtunik D, et al. EHR system MojTermin: implementation and initial data analysis. Stud Health Technol Inform. 2015;210:872–6.
9. Ministry of Health. Directorate for e-Health. National e-Health System. http://mojtermin.mk/health_workers. Accessed 01 Jun 2017.
10. Ministry of Health. Law on the Healthcare. Off J Repub Macedonia. 2015;10:12–88.
11. Ministry of Health. Guideline on healthcare related to the treatment and control of type 2 diabetes. Off J Repub Macedonia. 2015;40:15–34.
12. International Diabetes Federation. IDF diabetes Atlas. 8th ed. Brussels: International Diabetes Federation; 2017.
13. International Diabetes Federation. IDF diabetes Atlas. 9th ed. Brussels: International Diabetes Federation; 2019.
14. Golubnitschaja O, Kinkorova J, Costigliola V. Predictive, preventive and personalised medicine as the hardcore of 'Horizon 2020': EPMA position paper. EPMA J. 2014;5(1):6.
15. Golubnitschaja O, Costigliola V. European strategies in predictive, preventive and personalised medicine: highlights of the EPMA World Congress 2011. EPMA J. 2011;2(4):315–32.
16. Golubnitschaja O, Costigliola V. General report & recommendations in predictive, preventive and personalised medicine 2012: white paper of the European Association for Predictive, Preventive and Personalised Medicine. EPMA J. 2012;3(1):14.
17. Golubnitschaja O. Time for new guidelines in advanced healthcare: the mission of The EPMA journal to promote an integrative view in predictive, preventive and personalized medicine. EPMA J. 2012;3(1):5.
18. Smokovski I, Milenkovic T. First Metabolic Control Results in Insulin-Treated Diabetes Patients from Republic of Macedonia Derived from National eHealth System. Diabetes. 2019;68(Suppl 1):2393-PUB. https://doi.org/10.2337/db19-2393-PUB.
19. American Diabetes Association. Standards of medical care in diabetes 2020. Diabetes Care. 2020;43(1):s1–212.
20. Stone MA, Charpentier G, Doggen K, Kuss O, Lindblad U, et al. GUIDANCE Study Group. Quality of care of people with type 2 diabetes in eight European countries: findings from the Guideline Adherence to Enhance Care (GUIDANCE) study. Diabetes Care. 2013;36(9):2628–38.
21. Milenkovic T, Smokovski I, Kulumova E, Stojanovski N, Aleksov B. Significant improvement of glycemic control with BIAsp30 in clinical reality: experience from clinical practice in Macedonia. Diabetes. 2009;58(Suppl 1):2083.
22. Dimitrovski C, Smokovski I, Makrevska S, Mileva I, Kostojcinovska M. Significant improvements in glycemic control without weight gain with insulin detemir in clinical reality: experience from Macedonian clinical practice. Diabetes. 2009;58(Suppl 1):2084.
23. The Sixth Joint Task Force of the European Society of Cardiology and Other Societies on Cardiovascular Disease Prevention in Clinical Practice (constituted by representatives of 10 societies and by invited experts). 2016 European Guidelines on cardiovascular disease prevention in clinical practice. Eur Heart J. 2016;37:2315–2381.
24. Mihajlovska D, Smokovski I, Kocinski G, Bosevski M, Hristova E, et al. National prevalence of heart failure in type 2 diabetes patients derived from the National eHealth System and their access to treatment with SGLT2 Inhibitors or GLP-1 Receptor Agonists. 6th Macedonian Congress of Cardiology, 3–6 October 2019, Ohrid, Republic of North Macedonia.

Chapter 8
Promise of Nutrition

In the past three decades overweight and obesity replaced undernutrition as a major public healthcare challenge for the developing countries. Major changes in dietary patterns of developed countries were replicated later in the developing countries, including increased use of processed carbohydrates, especially in the form of beverages, inexpensive vegetable oils and animal-based diet. Urbanization and advances of technology in lower resource countries resulted in reduction of physical activity and have significantly contributed towards epidemiological transition and increased prevalence of diabetes.

Despite the emerging problem of overweight and obesity, parts of the population in some developing countries are still struggling with undernutrition, so the term 'twin malnutrition' reflects the both extremes of malnutrition: obesity and undernutrition [1]. More than a third of developing countries had overlapping forms of malnutrition, particularly in Sub-Saharan Africa, South Asia, and East Asia and the Pacific [1].

Consumption of carbohydrate containing sweeteners has considerably increased worldwide, and most of the food and beverages contain added sweeteners [2–4]. Majority of additional calories originating from added sweeteners are consumed through beverages. The excessive use of high-calorie drinks, stimulated by aggressive marketing from global companies especially towards youth, resulted in increasing rates of overweight and obesity as the critical drivers for diabetes. Additionally, the hectic lifestyle, insufficient time for cooking at home replaced by overconsumption of fast foods, added up to the increased calories intake and the diabetes tsunami [2].

Vegetable oils have become affordable for the majority of the population from developing countries, increasing their calories intake in a setting of low income. In the period between 1985 and 2010, individual intake of vegetable oils increased between three- to six fold in developing countries [2].

In addition, there has been considerable increase in the intake of animal-source foods in developing countries [5–7]. Excessive consumption of animal-source foods may be linked to the increase in the saturated fat intake and spiraling rates of

© Springer Nature Switzerland AG 2021
I. Smokovski, *Managing Diabetes in Low Income Countries*,
https://doi.org/10.1007/978-3-030-51469-3_8

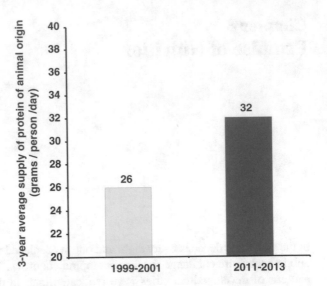

Fig. 8.1 Three year average supply of protein of animal origin in the Republic of North Macedonia, data adapted from Ref. [10]

obesity, diabetes, CVD and related mortality [8, 9]. Three year average supply of protein of animal origin in the Republic of North Macedonia increased from 26 grams per person per day in the period 1999–2001 to 32 grams per person per day in the period 2011–2013 (Fig. 8.1) [10].

Most of the affordable, processed foods contain trans-fats, another nutrient known to be associated with increased risk of cardiovascular events. High calorie fast foods are rich in trans-fats which additionally increases the risk of premature development of CVDs [11].

These unfavorable dietary trends in developing countries towards increased consumption of carbohydrates, vegetable oils and animal-sourced foods were paralleled with decreased consumption of legumes, vegetables and whole grains [2].

All these dietary patterns in developing countries only replicated what has already happened in large parts of population from developed countries. Traditionally, it has been reported that obesity and diabetes rates were higher in rural areas of developed countries, unlike the developing countries where those rates were generally higher in urban populations. However, recent trends suggest an increase in obesity and diabetes rates in rural populations of developing countries, similar to the patterns in developed countries [12]. The same has been found in the first stratified diabetes prevalence data derived from the NeHS in the Republic of North Macedonia, where the prevalence of diabetes was higher in rural compared to urban populations [13].

It has been reported that the burden of obesity and diabetes is greater in developing parts of the world, such as Asia, Latin America, Middle East, and Africa, which may be due to the differences in fat accumulation, and the cardiometabolic effects of BMI at levels below the threshold of 25 kg/m^2 [14].

Change of the nutritional pattern in the Republic of North Macedonia could be a striking example of its impact on the exponential rise of the national diabetes

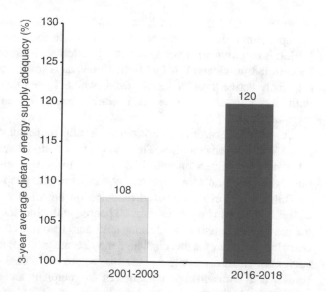

Fig. 8.2 Three year average dietary energy supply adequacy in the Republic of North Macedonia, data adapted from Ref. [10]

prevalence. Three year average dietary energy supply adequacy increased from 108% in the period 2001–2003 to 120% in the period 2016–2018 (Fig. 8.2) [10].

The increase of the calories intake in the Republic of North Macedonia reflects the similar trend in any developing country. Free movement of food supplies and affordable, processed foods rich in carbohydrates resulted in increase of obesity, insulin resistance, prediabetes and diabetes.

Not only the increased calories intake per person per day, but also the structure of the calories intake has been a strong driver for diabetes prevalence in the Republic of North Macedonia. It was mentioned that dietary habits in the Republic of North Macedonia have been very close to the population of Turkey, a country with the highest diabetes prevalence in Europe [13, 15].

Consumption of refined sugar in the Republic of North Macedonia increased considerably between 1991 and 1999 [15]. However, the consumption of sugar has remained high but steady since 1999 and could not account for all of the increased calories in diets [15]. Consumption of beef and veal have increased from 15 to 19 metric tons carcass weight equivalent, though not to the extent of swine and poultry consumption, both of which have more than doubled over this relatively short period [15]. These represent significant increases in the intake of saturated fat and cholesterol. Intake of sunflower seed oil, another high-fat, high-calorie food, has also more than doubled [15].

Nutrition recommendations for people with diabetes encourage reduced total calories and control of the quantity of carbohydrates as most important dietary interventions, together with the reduced intake of saturated fat [16, 17]. People have to be educated to recognize the carbohydrate content in different foods. Fortunately, nowadays, there are numerous online resources and mobile apps for identifying the nutritional content of the foods.

American Diabetes Association refers to the dietary patterns as medical nutrition therapy, emphasizing its therapeutic importance in diabetes and prediabetes care [16]. It is recommended that such dietary patterns are structured and communicated by certified providers. It is quite often nowadays to find many 'nutrition experts', especially active through social media, whose instructions are not always in line with the current evidence, and could result in dangerous acute diabetes complications.

Cases with uncertified 'nutritionists' are far more common in developing compared to developed countries. There has to be a national system with information of all certified providers on nutrition, in order to prevent dissemination of wrongful dietary information with tragic consequences for the people with diabetes.

Tailored and evidence based modules on nutrition are mandatory part of the SDEP, and have to be provided for all people with diabetes and prediabetes. Most of the developing countries are lacking sufficient resources for structured education on nutrition. Solution for this challenge may be the more prudent use of technologies, such as m-Health and online platforms, where accredited nutrition programs could be delivered with active participation of the recipient, and assessment of the knowledge attained after the program completion.

It has been demonstrated that education on nutrition has improved clinical outcomes, including improvement of glycaemic control, lipid profile and reduction of weight. In essence, it is a very powerful tool on par with the pharmacological intervention, and its value needs to be recognized by the healthcare systems of the developing countries.

Nutrition treatment and reduction of calories intake has to be a mandatory part of the diabetes care for overweight and obese people with a recommended gradual weight loss. Traditionally, there have been recommendations on calories distribution among macronutrients. Recent guidelines, however, do not support precise recommendation on distribution, emphasizing the individual approach and the requirement not to exceed the recommended calories intake per day.

It is not a single diet that is recommended, but a variety of eating patterns are acceptable for the management of type 2 diabetes and prediabetes, as well as for type 1 diabetes. Reduction of carbohydrates intake is generally recommended. Carbohydrates should preferably originate from minimally processed, high in fiber, nutrient-dense sources. Preferred sources of carbohydrates include non-starchy vegetables, whole grain, moderate consumption of fruits and dairy products [16].

Carbohydrate counting has been a critical skill for people with diabetes on insulin treatment, and is beneficial even for those on non-insulin treatments, or for people with prediabetes. Education is mandatory on the use of carbohydrate exchanges, reading food labels, and tailoring food choices. In addition, content of other macronutrients, such as fats and proteins, are important for people on insulin treatment in determining their mealtime insulin doses [16].

There are numerous mobile apps and online support that could facilitate the process of recognizing the amount of carbohydrates in various types of food. Those apps provide recording and tracking of calories intake, reports on distribution among macronutrients and servings, and could be of utmost importance for the user, but also for the healthcare provider.

There should be an absolute ban on the use of sugar-sweetened beverages in people with diabetes, and those should be substituted with water [16]. People with diabetes are recommended to consume coffee and tea without any added sugars [16]. If there is an urge for sugar intake, which is not caused by hypoglycemia, then it should be treated with low or no carbohydrate containing vegetables [16]. The UK has already introduced the so-called 'sugary drink tax' or 'soda tax' on sweetened beverages, which are considered to be one of the biggest drivers of obesity, especially in youth.

Some of the preferred diets for people with diabetes include Mediterranean and whole grain plant based diet. Mediterranean diet is rich in monounsaturated and polyunsaturated fats, and may be considered for improvement of glucose metabolism and lowering CVD risk [16]. Foods rich in long-chain, polyunsaturated fatty acids, such as n-3 fatty acids, found in fatty fish, nuts and seeds, are recommended for prevention of CVDs [16].

There is no clear evidence that dietary supplements with n-3, vitamins, minerals, vitamin D, herbs, or spices, such as cinnamon, can improve the glycaemic control in people with diabetes, and are, therefore, not recommended [16].

Under circumstances where drinking alcohol is socially acceptable, adults with diabetes are allowed to drink alcohol in moderation—no more than one drink per day for adult women, and no more than two drinks per day for adult men [16]. People who are drinking alcohol have to be educated on the signs, symptoms, and management of hypoglycemia, especially when using insulin or insulin secretagogues. It is critical to monitor glucose after drinking alcoholic beverages to reduce hypoglycemia risk [16].

People with diabetes and prediabetes should not exceed the sodium consumption of 2,300 mg/day, as for the general population [16]. Unfortunately, the sodium consumption in many developing countries is much higher, contributing to the increased prevalence of hypertension and CVDs [18]. Member states of WHO have agreed to reduce the intake of salt by 30% by 2025 [19, 20].

Another proposed strategy in terms of healthier nutrition has been the reduction of animal sourced products. A growing body of evidence suggests that use of a plant-based dietary pattern, with emphasis on whole grains, vegetables, legumes, fruits, and nuts, may offer significant advantages [15]. It has been reported that BMI and diabetes prevalence increase as the amount of animal products in the diet increases [15].

It has also been suggested that avoidance of any types of meat promoted longevity—vegetarian men who consume vegetables, legumes, grains, fruits, nuts, seeds, dairy products, and eggs, but no meat, lived 9.5 years longer, and vegetarian women lived 6.1 years longer than their meat-eating counterparts [15, 21].

In people diagnosed with type 2 diabetes, a vegan diet has been found to improve weight and plasma glucose values [15, 22]. Vegan and vegetarian diets have been reported to reduce cardiovascular risk factors, particularly blood pressure and cholesterol [15, 23, 24]. Furthermore, a plant-based dietary pattern with a very low (<10%) fat content was suggested to have potential of beneficially affecting the course of the coronary artery disease, the leading cause of death in people with diabetes [15, 25, 26].

After an analysis of almost 20 years of data that demonstrated effectiveness on the progression of coronary heart disease, reducing the need for coronary bypass surgery and percutaneous coronary interventions, the US Congress approved intensive dietary- and lifestyle-focused cardiac rehabilitation programs for Medicare recipients [15].

Many cardiovascular benefits of the plant-based diet have led the physicians to promote its adoption in people who have high cholesterol, diabetes, hypertension, or coronary artery disease [15]. It has recently been reported that men who consumed more plant-based foods over a 10-year period had a 25% reduced risk of heart disease, compared with those eating more animal-based foods, while for women the decrease was 11% [27]. However, the study found that people eating more unhealthful plant-based foods did not have a significantly lower risk of heart disease compared with people eating more animal-based foods [27].

A plant-based dietary pattern has been found to be acceptable for consuming by people with diabetes similarly to "conventional" diets [15, 28, 29]. Lower rates of a range of common cancers and improved cancer survival have also been reported among people on a plant-based diet [15, 30].

Perhaps of great interest for the developing countries is the evidence of the effectiveness of a plant-based dietary pattern to reduce the need for medication in people with type 2 diabetes. It has been demonstrated in a US study comparing a conventional diabetes diet with a low-fat, low glycaemic index, vegan dietary pattern, during the initial 22 weeks that 43% of participants reduced their diabetes medications, whereas 8% increased their medications [15, 22]. At 74 weeks, doses of medications for glycaemic control were reduced in 35% of participants, increased in 14%, and unchanged or mixed (changes in opposite directions in 2 medications) in the remainder [15, 22].

It has to be evaluated in developing countries if plant-based dietary intervention and moderate exercise could reduce the doses of diabetes medication for people with type 2 diabetes, including the insulin doses [15]. This intervention diet would focus on culturally familiar dishes made from legumes, vegetables, whole grains, fruits, nuts, and seeds, with generally recognized exercise requirements [15].

Such study could also include assessments of the intervention's acceptability and sustainability and would develop specific guidelines for reduction of insulin doses [15]. If shown to be effective in improving measures of health and reducing insulin requirements, this lifestyle intervention strategy could be adopted as a model for a diabetes intervention [15].

Average daily calories and carbohydrate exchanges, together with physical activity, should be recorded in the EHRs of the person with diabetes in order to track the BMI development as one of the critical parameters for adequate metabolic control. Such monitoring of BMI at individual level would allow monitoring of the prevalence of overweight and obesity at national level. It would be important to monitor BMI in people with diabetes, but also in people with prediabetes or even people with normoglycemia.

It should be mentioned that healthier food of domestically grown fruits and vegetables in developing countries could be less expensive than the processed, fast food. Recently a concept called 'Zero km food (0 km food)' was introduced [31]. This concept stands for food that is produced, sold and eaten locally, or the food that has travelled zero kilometers. It refers to non-industrial fruits, vegetables, honey, grains that are not transported through global trade chains; therefore, have no significant price margins and quality loss during long storage [31].

Another step in improving dietary patterns would be the broad use of food labels. Food labels could certainly help consumers make healthy choices. Labels with nutrition facts can help consumers compare similar foods and select those that are lower in salt, saturated and trans-fats, and added sugars. Food labels should be used by certified nutritionists to help consumers determine how many calories they should be consuming. Mobile apps are available that could provide all the required nutritional information by scanning the barcode of the packed foods.

Promotion of Mediterranean or whole grain plant based diet would actually mean going back to the roots of nutrition for the population in developing countries. Those are actually the foods their predecessors have been familiar with for ages.

In order to convey healthy dietary patterns to the population, the first activity should be to educate the educators. Similar to smoking, it would be difficult for a physician, nurse or diabetes educator who is smoking to request from individuals not to smoke. It is the same with the overweight or obese healthcare providers and for such purpose they need to be adequately educated and trained to modify their lifestyle, if needed.

Given the magnitude of the problem, there should be a mandatory curriculum in medical and related studies on nutrition with ability to gain practical skills in obtaining and preparing healthy food. The students and future providers have to know what is a healthy nutrition standard. In case of prediabetes and diabetes, nutrition would be equally important as pharmacological intervention. Medical schools around the globe should incorporate curriculums on nutrition in both undergraduate and postgraduate studies.

The potential exists for a much stronger role of nutrition in prevention and treatment of diabetes. Increasing the number of registered nurses with training in diabetes would benefit the general population and could reduce over-reliance on medication. Furthermore, certified and nationally accredited nutritionists have to be more actively involved in the management of diabetes.

Having in mind that it is very difficult to change the lifestyle of adults, education on nutrition has to begin as early as possible. Youth has to be taught about the high quality nutrition across all levels of education, and the process should be initiated as early as in the kindergartens. The education on nutrition should be paralleled with education on the importance of physical activity, and ample physical activities have to be a mandatory part of the formal education across all levels.

Developing countries have to produce guidelines on nutrition that would be broadly communicated to the general population. All the communication channels have to be deployed: mass media, online platforms, schools, universities, workplaces. Such activity has been implemented in the Republic of North Macedonia; where a Guideline on Nutrition has been published in 2014, followed by a communication campaign through various channels (Fig. 8.3) [32].

Насоките за исхрана на населението во Република Македонија претставуваат препораки за компонентите на

Fig. 8.3 Guideline on Nutrition from the Republic of North Macedonia [32]

Education and provision of healthy nutrients could be achieved in a setting with limited resources resulting in beneficial effects on the prevalence of obesity, diabetes and diabetes complications.

What needs to be done to maximize the promise of nutrition?
Each developing country should:

- …create and publish a Guideline on Nutrition to increase public awareness about healthy diet,
- …analyze the consumption of refined carbohydrates, oils and animal source food, and consider introducing 'sugary drink tax',
- … monitor individual BMI and national prevalence of overweight and obesity,
- …recognize proper nutrition as a critical component of diabetes management and for prevention of diabetes;
- …encourage reduction of carbohydrates intake, preferably from minimally processed, high in fiber, nutrient-dense sources,
- …consider ban on the use of trans-fats.

References

1. World Health Organization. More than one in three low- and middle-income countries face both extremes of malnutrition, 2019. https://www.who.int/news-room/detail/16-12-2019-more-than-one-in-three-low%2D%2Dand-middle-income-countries-face-both-extremes-of-malnutrition. Accessed 12 April 2020.
2. Popkin MB, Adair SL, Ng WS. Global nutrition transition and the pandemic of obesity in developing countries. Nutr Rev. 2011;70(1):3–21.
3. Popkin BM, Nielsen SJ. The sweetening of the world's diet. Obes Res. 2003;11:1325–32.
4. Duffey KJ, Popkin BM. High-fructose corn syrup: is this what's for dinner? Am J Clin Nutr. 2008;88(Suppl):S1722–32.
5. Delgado CL. Rising consumption of meat and milk in developing countries has created a new food revolution. J Nutr. 2003;133(Suppl):S3907–10.
6. Du S, Mroz TA, Zhai F, Popkin BM. Rapid income growth adversely affects diet quality in China – particularly for the poor! Soc Sci Med. 2004;59:1505–15.
7. Popkin BM, Du S. Dynamics of the nutrition transition toward the animal foods sector in China and its implications: a worried perspective. J Nutr. 2003;133(Suppl):S3898–906.
8. Sinha R, Cross AJ, Graubard BI, Leitzmann MF, Schatzkin A. Meat intake and mortality: a prospective study of over half a million people. Arch Intern Med. 2009;169:562–71.
9. Food and Agricultural Organization of the United Nations. Livestock's long shadow: environmental issues and options. Rome: Food and Agricultural Organization United Nations. 2007.
10. Food and Agriculture Organization of the United Nations. FAOStat, North Macedonia. http://www.fao.org/faostat/en/?#country/154. Accessed 12 April 2020.
11. World Health Organization. WHO plan to eliminate industrially-produced trans-fatty acids from global food supply. 2018. https://www.who.int/news-room/detail/14-05-2018-who-plan-to-eliminate-industrially-produced-trans-fatty-acids-from-global-food-supply. Accessed 24 March 2020.
12. Jones-Smith JC, Gordon-Larsen P, Siddiqi A, Popkin BM. Emerging disparities in overweight by educational attainment in Chinese adults (1989–2006). Int J Obes (London). 2011; https://doi.org/10.1038/ijo.2011.134.
13. Smokovski I, Milenkovic T, Cho HN. First stratified diabetes prevalence data for Republic of Macedonia derived from the National eHealth System. Diabetes Res Clin Pract. 2018;143:179–83.
14. Nguyen TT, Adair LS, Suchindran CM, He K, Popkin BM. The association between body mass index and hypertension is different between East and Southeast Asians. Am J Clin Nutr. 2009;89:1905–12.
15. Smokovski I, Milenkovic T, Trapp C, Mitov A. Diabetes care in the Republic of Macedonia: challenges and opportunities. Ann Global Health. 2015;81(6):792–802.
16. American Diabetes Association. Standards of medical care in diabetes 2020. Diabetes Care. 2020;43(1):s1–212.
17. Thorpe CT, Fahey LE, Johnson H, Deshpande M, Thorpe JM, et al. Facilitating healthy coping in patients with diabetes: a systematic review. Diabetes Educ. 2013;39:33–52.
18. World Health Organization. Elliott P, Brown I. Sodium intakes around the world. Background document prepared for the Forum and Technical meeting on Reducing Salt Intake in Populations, 2007.
19. World Health Organization. Healthy diet. https://www.who.int/who-documents-detail/healthy-diet-factsheet394. Accessed 13 April 2020.
20. World Health Organization. Noncommunicable diseases: Campaign for action – meeting the NCD targets. Know the NCD targets. https://www.who.int/beat-ncds/take-action/targets/en/. Accessed 10 April 2020.
21. Orlich MJ, Singh PN, Sabate J, et al. Vegetarian dietary patterns and mortality in Adventist Health Study-2. JAMA Intern Med. 2013;173:1230e8.

22. Barnard ND, Cohen J, Jenkins DJ, et al. A low-fat vegan diet and a conventional diabetes diet in the treatment of type 2 diabetes: a randomized, controlled 74-week clinical trial. Am J Clin Nutr. 2009;89(Suppl):1588Se96S.

23. Yokoyama Y, Nishimura K, Barnard ND, et al. Vegetarian diets and blood pressure: a meta-analysis. JAMA Intern Med. 2014;174:577e87.

24. Ferdowsian HR, Barnard ND. Effects of plant-based diets on plasma lipids. Am J Cardiol. 2009;104:947e56.

25. Ornish D, Scherwitz LW, Billings JH, et al. Intensive lifestyle changes for reversal of coronary heart disease. JAMA. 1998;280:2001e7.

26. Esselstyn CB Jr, Ellis SG, Medendorp SV, et al. A strategy to arrest and reverse coronary artery disease: a 5-year longitudinal study of a single physician's practice. J Fam Pract. 1995;41:560e8.

27. American College of Cardiology. To Reap Heart Benefits of a Plant-Based Diet, Avoid Junk Food. Plant-based diet found to reduce cardiovascular risk, but only if foods are healthful Mar 18, 2020. https://www.acc.org/about-acc/pressreleases#sort=%40foriginalz32xpostedz32xd ate90022%20descending. Accessed 09 April 2020.

28. Craig WJ, Mangels AR. Position of the American Dietetic Association: vegetarian diets. J Am Diet Assoc. 2009;109:1266e82.

29. Barnard ND, Gloede L, Cohen J, et al. A low-fat vegan diet elicits greater macronutrient changes, but is comparable in adherence and acceptability, compared with a more conventional diabetes diet among individuals with type 2 diabetes. J Am Diet Assoc. 2009;109:263e72.

30. Ferdowsian H, Barnard ND. The role of diet in breast and prostate cancer survival. Ethn Dis. 2007;17(2 Suppl 2). S2e18–22.

31. Sustainability Network: Zero km food. 2014. https://sustainetwork.wordpress.com/2014/01/15/ zero-km-food/. Accessed 11 April 2020.

32. Ministry of Health. Guidelines on Nutrition of the population of the Republic of Macedonia, http://zdravstvo.gov.mk/vodich-za-ishrana/.Accessed 10 April 2020.

Chapter 9
Focus on Diabetes Prevention

Developing countries are at much higher risk of going bankrupt if diabetes or diabetes complications are not prevented. Previous chapters were discussing the various aspects and possibilities to prevent diabetes and its complications. Those activities should be based on knowing the magnitude of the problem by determining the prevalence of diagnosed and undiagnosed diabetes cases. Although the global estimates reported for a particular country are based on sound methods, sometimes the results from a local study could give surprising results, as each country has its own specifics.

Mapping of available health care resources dedicated to diabetes care is critical to realize if they are sufficient across healthcare levels and geographical coverage, or to compensate for age transition and migration to developed countries for better paid jobs. National Program of Residencies and Fellowships has to be in place, at least for a 4 years period, as it is not possible to produce Endocrinologists and Diabetologists in a short period of time (Fig. 9.1) [1]. Age of physicians involved in diabetes care needs to be monitored closely for smooth transition of retired staff.

The number of residencies and fellowships for Endocrinologists and Diabetologists in the Republic of North Macedonia was increased by 20% in the period 2015–2016. Plans should also be available for other healthcare providers involved in diabetes care. National plans covering healthcare resources have to be updated at least on an annual basis.

In the most affected developing countries diabetes has to be brought up very high on the political agenda, otherwise it would not be possible to provide the required resources to implement the nationwide policies. Political support is necessary for implementation of activities to prevent diabetes and its complications. Medical community and scientific associations could initiate dialogue with political leaders and offer solutions; however, there has to be a strong political will for the country-wide measures to be implemented.

The example of Republic of North Macedonia confirms the importance of political support in designating diabetes as a specific medical condition in the laws [2]. If the regulatory infrastructure is in place, in addition to the National Diabetes

© Springer Nature Switzerland AG 2021
I. Smokovski, *Managing Diabetes in Low Income Countries*,
https://doi.org/10.1007/978-3-030-51469-3_9

30 април 2015   *Службен весник*   Бр. 69 - Стр. 5
на Република Македонија

2417.

Врз основа на член 148 став 1 од Законот за здравствената заштита („Службен весник на Република Македонија" бр. 43/12, 145/12, 87/13, 164/13, 39/14, 43/14, 132/14, 188/14 и 10/15), Владата на Република Македонија, на седницата, одржана на 22.04.2015 година, донесе

ПРОГРАМА
ЗА ПОТРЕБИТЕ ОД СПЕЦИЈАЛИСТИЧКИ И СУПСПЕЦИЈАЛИСТИЧКИ КАДРИ СОГЛАСНО СО МРЕЖАТА НА ЗДРАВСТВЕНИ УСТАНОВИ (2015 – 2018)

1. Со оваа програма се утврдува потребата од специјалистички и супспецијалистички кадри за секоја година посебно во период од 2015 – 2018 година.

-I-

ПРОГРАМА ЗА ПОТРЕБИТЕ ОД СПЕЦИЈАЛИСТИЧКИ И СУПСПЕЦИЈАЛИСТИЧКИ КАДРИ СОГЛАСНО СО МРЕЖАТА НА ЗДРАВСТВЕНИ УСТАНОВИ ЗА 2015 ГОДИНА

1. ЈЗУ Универзитетска клиника за урологија – Скопје

СПЕЦИЈАЛИЗАЦИЈА		
1.	Урологија	1

2. ЈЗУ Универзитетска клиника за трауматологија, ортопедски болести, анестезија, реанимација, интензивно лекување и ургентен центар - Скопје

СПЕЦИЈАЛИЗАЦИЈА		
1.	Анестезиологија со интензивно лекување	3
2.	Ортопедија	1
3.	Ургентна медицина	3
СУПСПЕЦИЈАЛИЗАЦИЈА		
1.	Педијатриска анестезиологија	6
2.	Трауматологија на остеоартикуларен систем	5

3. ЈЗУ Универзитетска клиника за нефрологија – Скопје

СУПСПЕЦИЈАЛИЗАЦИЈА		
1.	Нефрологија	3

Fig. 9.1 National Program of Residencies and Fellowships published in the Official Journal of the Republic of North Macedonia [1]

Plan, National Diabetes Care guidelines and the NeHS, there has to be a national body accountable for the implementation of activities and monitoring of adherence (Fig. 7.3) [3–7].

That body, National Diabetes Committee, has to be stipulated in the laws to have executive power and accountability [2]. It should be responsible for overseeing the situation with diabetes care in the country, and for planning of future activities. Those activities might include more Endocrinologists, more Diabetes Centers, more insulin pharmacies, evaluation of cost-effectiveness of current and introduction of novel diabetes treatments or glucose monitoring technologies. The National Diabetes Committee has to be composed of high-level experts with integrity and no conflicts of interest.

All the activities, plans, timelines related to diabetes care in the country have to be consolidated in a National Diabetes Plan, a strategic document endorsed by the highest political levels. Such document could be developed by the National Diabetes

Committee, but has to be backed by the Ministry of Health and the Government. It should be a live document that is continuously updated.

The most important tool for the National Diabetes Committee would be the NeHS with its numerous possibilities of generating analysis and reports (Figs. 7.1 and 7.2) [4, 5, 7]. There are many disadvantages for small developing countries affected by the diabetes pandemic. One of the advantages is that all the aforementioned steps could be implemented in a relatively short period of time, if there is a strong political will and support by the medical community. The Republic of North Macedonia is an example that all the steps could be achieved in a setting with limited resources.

When such systemic approach is undertaken, main diabetes drivers in the country need to be identified, such as overweight, obesity, prediabetes, smoking and GDM. Activities to curb the drivers have to be described in the National Diabetes Plan.

Diabetes is a very costly disease exerting huge pressure on the healthcare budgets of both developed and developing countries. Unfortunately, many countries spend most of their healthcare resources on treating complications, and not on prevention. It is critical to shift the paradigm towards diabetes prevention. Such change has to come initially from the medical community, and to be conveyed to the policy makers afterwards. Otherwise, it would be difficult to implement nationwide measures, especially in a relatively healthy population not diagnosed with any NCD at the time being.

Both developed and developing countries have to be focused on the prevention of diabetes and diabetes complications in order to prevent bankruptcy of their healthcare systems. Even in the developed countries, it is estimated that more than one third of people with diabetes are not receiving the recommended care that helps prevent complications. This share is much higher in developing countries. Unfortunately, the latest COVID-19 global pandemic would urge even the most developed countries to look for creative solutions for managing the rising diabetes costs.

If main modifiable diabetes drivers are identified, efforts should be directed towards prevention and management of these conditions. Understandably, in order to manage it you have to measure it first. Therefore, the prevalence of diabetes drivers has to be estimated. If the parameters such as BMI, smoking status, or prediabetes are recorded in the EHRs, it would be relatively easy to estimate the prevalence from the NeHS and to target the affected population.

Another step would be to set nation-specific targets for curbing the prevalence of drivers in the SMART manner; i.e. the targets have to be Specific, Measurable, Achievable, Realistic and Time-bound. One example could be the reduction of obesity by 5% on an annual basis, which should be monitored by the National Diabetes Committee from the NeHS. All these activities and targets have to be specified in the National Diabetes Plan.

In creating national targets for prevention of diabetes and related complications, the WHO Global NCD Targets could be used as a reference, and adjusted according to the local circumstances [8]. Those targets include relative reduction of premature death from NCDs by 25% by2025, at least 10% relative reduction in the harmful use of alcohol, at least 10% relative reduction in prevalence of insufficient physical activity, 30% relative reduction in sodium intake, 30% relative reduction in prevalence of current tobacco use, 25% relative reduction in the prevalence of hypertension, halting the rise of diabetes and obesity, at least 50% of eligible people to receive drug therapy and counseling (including glycaemic control) to prevent heart attacks and strokes, and an 80% availability of the affordable basic technologies and essential medicines, including generics, required to treat NCDs [8].

Education on healthy nutrition for the general population has to start as early as possible, even in the kindergarten. And such dietary patterns, accompanied by obtaining skills in preparing healthy food, have to be taught throughout all levels of education. Avoiding carbohydrate rich beverages, processed carbohydrates, or adding carbohydrates rich sweeteners, should be a community standard in order to prevent the rising obesity prevalence in children and adolescents.

It has been reported that carbohydrate rich beverages are the main source of carbohydrate ingestion leading to obesity and diabetes, especially in youth. Some developed countries, such as the UK, have introduced the so-called 'sugary drink tax' or 'soda tax', as a tax on sweetened beverages aiming to reduce the consumption of drinks with added sugar. Such initiative or a similar one taxing the 'junk food' could certainly be replicated in developing countries.

Another area that could significantly contribute to the reduction of atherosclerosis and CVDs is the ban on trans-fats. The ban has already been imposed in certain developed countries, including Denmark, Switzerland, Canada, the UK and the US. Although global food companies have reduced the amount of trans-fats in developed countries, they have not been banned in most of the developing countries.

The WHO announced an ambitious plan to eliminate the use of trans-fats worldwide, including the industrially produced edible oil for making margarine that have been linked to millions of premature cardiovascular deaths [9]. Although artificial trans-fats, or partially hydrogenated vegetable oil, have contributed to a half million deaths annually, many of developing countries are not prepared to address this health challenge [9].

It was mentioned that each developing country should have its own Guidelines on Nutrition (Fig. 8.3) [10]. Those should be communicated broadly to the general population through all available channels. The Guidelines have to be jointly developed by various Ministries, including those responsible for Health, Education, and Economy. They have to be implemented for the preparation of meals for children in kindergarten and throughout all levels of education. Such Guidelines could include banning machines for beverages or candies inside or close to the schools and universities. As already emphasized, if the habits for a healthy diet are not gained at an earliest age, it is extremely difficult to modify them later throughout life.

People preparing the food in kindergarten and schools have to be educated on the requirements of the National Guidelines on Nutrition, and have to adhere to those requirements. They should be encouraged to use a lot of vegetables and fruits, and in some cases to select certain spices that would make the food appealing to the children.

In many cases teachers have to be involved in the train-the-trainer education. If the teachers are overweight or obese, and they are the role models for the pupils, it would be very difficult to teach the children on a healthy nutrition.

In other instances, the parents of affected children have to be involved, as children are usually a reflection of the parents' habits or lifestyle. It would be more productive if education on nutrition is jointly attended by both parents and children. Resources to guide them for preparation of healthy food could be in various forms, including mobile apps, online platforms, or brochures.

Homework for children could include preparing a healthy dish with their parents, or completion of certain physical activity, in addition to doing math and science. Despite aggressive marketing campaigns of global food chains, children should be discouraged to consume unhealthy snacks, neither sweet nor salty, and should be taught to use vegetables or fruits as a snack instead.

The menus in all restaurants have to provide nutritional and calories value of the choices offered, so the customers would be familiar with the information before ordering the type and quantity of the food.

Monitoring of overweight and obesity in children is of particular importance due to the rising prevalence of type 2 diabetes at an earlier age. Children and the total population should be encouraged to use bikes as a means of transportation, thereby increasing their physical activity.

One way of promoting such a healthy lifestyle could be to assign prominent public figures who are physically active, lean, and non-smokers, as 'Ambassadors of Healthy Lifestyle'. They could be used as lifestyle role models for the entire population.

It is recommended that people with diabetes should practice at least 60 min per day of moderate- or vigorous-intensity aerobic activity, spread over at least 3 days per week, with no more than 2 consecutive days without activity [11]. Shorter durations of minimum 75 min per week of vigorous intensity or interval training could be adequate for younger and physically prepared individuals [11]. Adults with diabetes should have at least 2–3 sessions of resistance exercise per week on non-consecutive days [11].

Although the above recommendations are directed towards people with diabetes, they are also relevant for the people with no diabetes. Developing countries should consider increasing the hours of physical activity of preschool and school population at all ages, accompanied with theoretical support of the benefits of increased physical activity. In addition, facilities for physical activities have to be provided at schools, universities, workplaces or neighborhoods.

The lockdown imposed in times of global pandemics, such as the recent one with COVID-19, presents additional challenge for the physical activities desperately needed for regulation of glycaemia. Even under such circumstances, people with diabetes should be encouraged to be physically active.

Mobile technologies and apps could be very useful in keeping track of the daily calories intake and physical activity. They also provide opportunities to share the data with the healthcare providers for analysis, discussion and mutual agreement on the further steps. As such, they are great resources for diabetes prevention, or improvement of metabolic control in people with diabetes to prevent complications.

When the NeHS is in place, the data on calories intake and physical activity should also be recorded in the individual EHRs for monitoring of the modifiable risk factors for diabetes.

Furthermore, comprehensive national programs for smoking cessations have to be in place, as smoking has been identified as one of the risk factors for development of diabetes, and a major risk factor for CVDs. Activities should include smoke-free work and other public places, spending on public information campaigns, comprehensive bans on advertising and promotion, large direct health warning labels, and absolute ban for selling cigarettes to minors.

It is very important that above measures are accompanied by considerable increase in prices of cigarettes, making them less affordable for the general population. Another measure could be to drastically increase the contribution to healthcare insurance fund if a person is a smoker, compared to a non-smoker. All these initiatives have already worked effectively in developed countries, and could certainly be implemented in developing countries.

Developing countries should be advised against the use of cigarettes and other tobacco products, or e-cigarettes [12]. The legal status of e-cigarettes is currently pending in many countries, and the list of countries banning the use of e-cigarettes is getting longer. Fortunately, many developing countries are implementing activities against smoking cigarettes, tobacco, or e-cigarettes.

After identification of tobacco or e-cigarette use, smoking cessation counseling has to be implemented in addition to other forms of treatment as a routine component of diabetes care. Initiatives for reduction or quitting of smoking could use the 5A Concept, A (Ask)—always ask about current smoking status; A (Advise)—unambiguously advise all smokers to quit smoking; A (Assess)—assess the level of dependency and preparedness to quit smoking; A (Assist)—assist with behavioral and pharmacological support if needed, agreeing when to quit smoking with a precise date; A (Arrange)—arrange the next follow-up visit to monitor the progress of quitting smoking [13].

In addition to overweight and obesity, prediabetes should primarily be targeted to prevent progression into type 2 diabetes. People diagnosed with prediabetes have to be monitored, although many of them would not be pharmacologically treated. It is very important to address preventive activities towards this vulnerable population, as it is estimated that one third of people with prediabetes progress to diabetes, one third remain in prediabetes, and one third could convert into normoglycemia. This condition is independently associated with increased cardiovascular risk even prior to the diagnosis of diabetes, which only emphasizes the importance of its management.

People with prediabetes need to be considered for intensive lifestyle intervention programs based on the DPPs to achieve and maintain weight loss. Combination of aerobic and resistance training is preferred for prevention of diabetes.

Recommended lifestyle for reducing diabetes risk should include diet with no more than 30% of daily energy from fat; no more than 10% of energy from saturated fat; at least 10% of monounsaturated fatty acids, at least 20 g of fiber per 1,000 kcal; at least 30 min per day of moderate physical activity; and at least 5% weight reduction annually [13].

Excessive calories intake has to be avoided in people with prediabetes and replaced with reduced calories intake and reduced intake of carbohydrates. Vitamins or micronutrient supplementation are not recommended for prevention of diabetes, if there is no underlying deficiency.

The initial treatment for diabetes, metformin, could be considered in people with prediabetes, especially for those with BMI > 35 kg/m^2, age over 60 years, and women with prior GDM [11]. Prediabetes is associated with increased CVD risk; therefore, screening for modifiable risk factors for CVD and their treatment is highly recommended. Structured education programs may be appropriate for people with prediabetes, particularly the modules on nutrition and physical activity.

The main goal of people already diagnosed with diabetes is to prevent diabetes complications. Adequate glycaemic control is crucial in prevention of microvascular and macrovascular complications. The glycaemic control should be monitored through the individual EHRs from NeHS, enabling the monitoring at a national level.

Very important step in prevention of diabetes complications is early diagnosis of diabetes. That could be done only after thorough assessment of diabetes risk factors, or by using diabetes risk tools, and testing for diabetes in identified high-risk individuals.

Benchmarks could be implemented to identify hospitals that are achieving targets in glycaemic control, or in other metabolic parameters. Those benchmarks could serve for incentives of physicians achieving better results, but also for the people with diabetes to be aware of the quality of care they receive in different hospitals.

Indicators and targets for prediabetes and diabetes could be included in the Balanced Score Card system for evaluation of the overall performance of healthcare institutions, where the remuneration and bonuses for the management and the healthcare workers would be linked to the achievement of the targets.

The NeHS could be used as a platform for prevention of diabetes, through monitoring of people with prediabetes or other diabetes drivers. The NeHS can be used for monitoring the development of diabetes complications, but also if the physicians are adhering to the frequency of screening for diabetes complications, as recommended by the National Diabetes Care guidelines. It could be considered that part of remuneration of physicians is based on achieving certain diabetes related indicators reflecting adequate metabolic control and management of diabetes complications.

Psychosocial stress should not be neglected as an important driver for development of diabetes, and for worsening of glycaemic control in people with diabetes. Physical activity could be helpful for alleviating the psychosocial stress in many instances. In more severe cases, professional support has to be offered.

It was mentioned that these nationwide initiatives require top-level political support in order to be implemented. Many initiatives were undertaken in the Republic of North Macedonia, a developing, European country with limited resources.

However, continuity is necessary for implementation of such initiatives, as results are not immediately visible and politicians in many developing countries usually think only until the next elections.

Some of these initiatives could be quick wins or produce short- to mid-term results, but the majority of initiatives stipulated in the National Diabetes Plan produce results and benefits for the society in the long-term. One of the challenges for developing countries is the lack of continuity of nationwide initiatives, when it comes to change of political leadership.

Diabetes tsunami is coming in developing countries with its whole complexity. However, by introducing some of the proposed initiatives there is a possibility for providing sustainable diabetes care with favorable outcomes even in a setting with limited resources.

What could be done to prevent diabetes and is complications?
Each developing country should…

- … maintain a National Program of Residencies and Fellowships in Endocrinology and Diabetes,
- …shift the paradigm and more resources towards diabetes prevention,
- …monitor modifiable risk factors for development of diabetes, and metabolic control for prevention of diabetes complications,
- …implement Guidelines on Nutrition for the general population, and across all levels of education, starting as early as in kindergarten,
- …increase physical activity for the general population, and across all levels of education;
- …ensure continuity of initiatives stipulated in the National Diabetes Plan if there is a change of political leadership.

References

1. Ministry of Health. Program for the required Residences and Fellowships according to the Network of Healthcare Institutions, 2015–2018. Off J Repub Macedonia. 2015;69:5–49.
2. Ministry of Health. Law on Healthcare. Off J Repub Macedonia. 2015;10:12–88.
3. Ministry of Health. Guideline on healthcare related to the treatment and control of type 2 diabetes. Off J Repub Macedonia. 2015;40:15–34.
4. Smokovski I, Milenkovic T, Cho HN. First stratified diabetes prevalence data for Republic of Macedonia derived from the National eHealth System. Diabetes Res Clin Pract. 2018;143:179–83.
5. Smokovski I, Milenkovic T, Trapp C, Mitov A. Diabetes care in the Republic of Macedonia: challenges and opportunities. Ann Global Health. 2015;81(6):792–802.
6. Health Consumer Powerhouse. Euro health consumer index report, 2014. Taby, Sweden: Health Consumer Powerhouse. 2015. https://healthpowerhouse.com/media/EHCI-2014/EHCI-2014-report.pdf. Accessed 20 March 2020.
7. Velinov G, Jakimovski B, Lesovski D, Ivanova Panova D, Frtunik D, et al. EHR system MojTermin: implementation and initial data analysis. Stud Health Technol Inform. 2015;210:872–6.

8. World Health Organization. Noncommunicable diseases: Campaign for action – meeting the NCD targets. Know the NCD targets. https://www.who.int/beat-ncds/take-action/targets/en/. Accessed 10 April 2020.
9. World Health Organization. WHO plan to eliminate industrially-produced trans-fatty acids from global food supply, 14 May 2018. https://www.who.int/news-room/detail/14-05-2018-who-plan-to-eliminate-industrially-produced-trans-fatty-acids-from-global-food-supply. Accessed 10 April 2020.
10. Ministry of Health. Guidelines on Nutrition of the population of the Republic of Macedonia, 2020. http://zdravstvo.gov.mk/vodich-za-ishrana/. Accessed 10 April 2020.
11. American Diabetes Association. Standards of medical care in diabetes 2020. Diabetes Care. 2020;43(1):s1–212.
12. World Health Organization. E-cigarettes. https://www.who.int/news-room/q-a-detail/e-cigarettes-how-risky-are-they. Accessed 10 April 2020.
13. The Sixth Joint Task Force of the European Society of Cardiology and Other Societies on Cardiovascular Disease Prevention in Clinical Practice (constituted by representatives of 10 societies and by invited experts). 2016 European Guidelines on cardiovascular disease prevention in clinical practice. Eur Heart J. 2016;37:2315–81.

Index

© Springer Nature Switzerland AG 2021
I. Smokovski, *Managing Diabetes in Low Income Countries*,
https://doi.org/10.1007/978-3-030-51469-3